THE
COLONIAL
WORLD

THE WORLD OF LATIN AMERICA SERIES
Kenneth J. Grieb, Consulting Editor

THE COLONIAL WORLD OF LATIN AMERICA
John Francis Bannon
Saint Louis University

THE BRAZILIAN WORLD
Robert A. Hayes
Texas Tech University

──────────────COMING IN 1983──────────────

THE MEXICAN WORLD
Kenneth J. Grieb
University of Wisconsin-Oshkosh

THE ANDEAN WORLD
Lawrence A. Clayton
University of Alabama

──────────────COMING IN 1984──────────────

THE SOUTHERN CONE OF LATIN AMERICA
William F. Sater
California State University–Long Beach

THE CARIBBEAN AND CENTRAL AMERICAN WORLD
Louis A. Pérez, Jr.
University of South Florida

THE
COLONIAL
WORLD
OF LATIN AMERICA

John Francis Bannon

FORUM PRESS

Cover Design by Tom Heggie
Maps by Dan Irwin

Published simultaneously in Canada.

Printed in the United States of America.

Library of Congress Catalog Card Number: 81-69334

ISBN: 0-88273-601-9

Contents

Introduction

Latin America. The area of the Western Hemisphere stretching southeastward from the Florida Strait and into the Caribbean on the one side and from the Mexican-United States border and the Rio Grande on the other is known as Latin America—the more northerly reaches of the hemisphere make up Anglo America. Thus Latin America comprises the southerly extension of North America and the entire South American continent, along with the island-dotted Caribbean. In the area are found some twenty nations, including several having been recently added to the traditional list.

Latin America's geography is vast, rich, and varied, considerably greater in square-mileage than the Anglo American area. Its mountains include Mexico's twin Sierra Madre ranges, the line of volcanoes stretching through the Central American strip toward the land bridge between the continents, the Isthmus of Panama, then the rugged, majestic, towering Andean cordillera running the full length of the southern continent, and to the east the sprawling Brazilian Highland.

The southern continent has its great river systems. The Orinoco runs through the northern plains, the great Amazon drains the tropical belt, flowing from the cordillera eastward to the Atlantic, the Río de la Plata system waters the lush southern plains, the Magdalena, not nearly as large or extended as the others, still is important for the northwest high country.

Latin America has its full share of climates, ranging from the subtropical in the north to the full fury of the equatorial belt to another subtropical stretch to a temperate zone fusing into the subarctic in Tierra del Fuego. Well over half of Latin America lies between the Tropics Cancer and Capricorn. Through the tropical belt life can only be comfortable when man sets his towns and cities high in the mountains, to find at such elevations temperate living which the next zone southward affords automatically. This is a key factor in the region's development and explains the placement of the principal cities and power centers.

Latin America's subsoil is very rich. While the Spaniards were interested only in its gold, silver, and mercury, the area later yielded a fantastic store of other metals and minerals, copper and tin, iron ore of fine quality, the nonferrous metals in abundance, and most recently that "black gold" which is petroleum. The area includes vast deserts and great forests, as well as some of the finest bread-basket plains of all the world, which are also most hospitable stretches in which to raise stock.

Latin American History. If one holds to the strict definition that history is the story of humankind as reconstructed from written records, then Latin American history is something relatively new, dating only from that October day in 1492 when Christopher Columbus and eighty-nine sea-weary companions stumbled ashore on the little island in the Bahama chain. From their newly christened San Salvador (now Watling's Island) they sailed southward and found more islands. Next, most of them went back home to report. Within a matter of months more subjects of Isabella of Castile, Columbus' sponsor, were sailing west to lay the foundations of a Spanish empire overseas. Materials for the historical record began to accumulate.

However, unwritten records of humans in the Americas prior to 1492 had been piling up for many thousands of years. This so-called prehistory merits some notice and attention.

1

The Pre-1492 Americans

As they spread through the Caribbean and onto the mainland of the two continents, the Spaniards, and other Europeans who followed them, found that wherever they touched men were there before them. Columbus in 1492, convinced that he had reached his goal, the Indies of the East, named the first men whom he found Indians. Though a misnomer this name continues to designate the native Americans.

● The Indians: Who? Whence? When? How?

In the absence of formal written records, moderns have to rely on data furnished by a variety of specialists, anthropologists and archaeologists, ethnographers, paleontologists, geologists, and others. Piecing bits together moderns feel secure in tracing human prehistory in the Western Hemisphere back many thousands of years, maybe even as far back as 25,000 years or more; all postulate at least 10,000 years. Since no respected opinion holds for the Americas as the place of human origin, the Indians have to be immigrants.

Majority opinion, on the basis of extensive somatic comparisons, sees the Indians as members of the Mongoloid race of men, like the Chinese, and, therefore, Asiatic in origin and migrants from that continent. Admitting other slim possibilities, the moderns feel that the largest majority of the ancestors of the early "Americans" came into the Western Hemisphere via the Bering Strait entry, either over the land bridge which seems to have joined the two continents at that point during the Ice Age, or over the short ice-blocked water passage of a later date. Thence, through the succeeding millennia the descendants of the early immigrants spread through the two American continents and differentiated into the hundreds of subgroups found by the Europeans from Arctic north to Antarctic south.

When man came is more difficult to determine. However, on the basis of culture traits reported by the first European observers and the universal absence of others, the immigrations would seem to have taken place at least ten thousand years ago. They clearly predated such advances in the Old World as the domestication of horses and cattle, and such cereals as wheat, none of which were found in even the most advanced American civilizations.

By taking the universal common denominators among the culture traits reported by the first European observers some key to the original culture baggage can be found. For instance, Indians everywhere had stone and bone tools, the spear and the bow-and-arrow, family groupings, puberty rites, and more. Whatever else was found should be credited to later individual or regional ingenuity.

● The Major Indian Civilizations

Three such civilizations had developed in Latin America by the time the Europeans arrived, and a fourth was making advances.

The Maya civilization was the first of these to develop, turning the steaming jungles of Central America and southern Mexico into fertile fields that supported extensive city states of considerable population. This required effective social organization and specialization of labor, as well as control, and the ability to direct great numbers of workers over the long periods of time needed to construct immense temples, cities, and water reservoirs capable of holding millions of gallons of collected rainwater, and the power too to organize a farming enterprise capable of supporting a class of artisans, specialists, and governors. A complex religion provided the sinews which held the society together and enabled its rise. Most of its leaders were wise men and scholars who wielded both civil and religious authority. The massive monuments constructed to their many gods emphasize the skill and dedication of the Maya as well as the stability of their social structure. Besides engineers the class of scholars included astronomers who produced a calendar more accurate than the Julian calendar then in use in

Europe, and mathematicians who had arrived at the concept of the zero. The Maya civilization was in definite decline at the time of the coming of the Spaniards.

In Mexico, the Aztecs, the latest in a long series of invaders from the north, built an imposing culture on the skills and knowledge of their predecessors. They eventually established an extensive empire in central Mexico based on tribute, that is, one which they did not fully govern but rather one from which they received produce, goods, and taxes. They, too, had their scholars, engineers, and a priestly caste serving a complex polytheistic religion which at times practiced human sacrifice. Their central area was densely populated and quite urbanized. Their capital city, Tenochtitlán, astounded the Spaniards who found it larger than cities in Europe, constructed on islands in a great lake, connected to the shore by causeways, supplied with fresh water through long aqueducts, and containing huge temple complexes, pyramids, and lavish carvings.

High in the Andes of Peru the Inca established another civilization and a true empire, which was centrally governed from its capital of Cuzco by an emperor quite as powerful as many a European monarch. Social and societal organization were much more rigid in the Inca empire, reflecting the harsh climate and the limited water and tillable land available. The area was controlled early by warlike societies, essential to allocation of land and survival. The Inca eventually ruled the region of highland and coast from Ecuador to northern Chile. Mirroring their region, the cities were somewhat smaller than those of Middle America. They directed their building efforts to developing an elaborate network of roads and strong fortresses built on the mountain heights. Their public buildings were somewhat modest. They never developed a system of writing comparable to that of the Maya and the Aztecs, yet they were able to keep accurate count of inhabitants and resources. They maintained communication by a system of runners, constructed irrigation systems, and set up storehouses for grain that supplied government and populace and protected against drought.

The list of Indian accomplishments could go on. However, even the greatest of these native civilizations had, by European standards at least, serious deficiencies. Most notably, they did not know iron or even bronze for their tools, did not have the wheel or domesticated draft animals, and lacked knowledge of most useful grains and cereals.

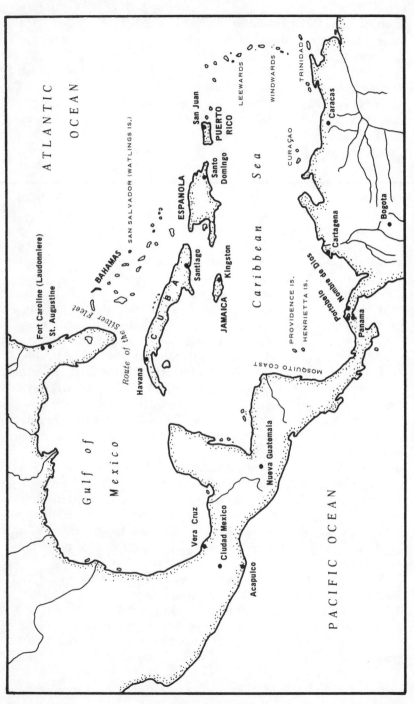

MEXICO AND THE CIRCUM-CARIBBEAN AREA

2

Discovery and Conquest

● A New World for Europeans

In late summer of 1492 Columbus sailed out of Palos in Spain to test the validity of his conviction that Calicut and Cathay, those fabled lands of the East, could be reached by a western route. Men of Europe, notably the articulate Marco Polo of Venice, had earlier gone overland to the kingdom of the Great Khan of China and returned to tell Europeans of its astounding sights and riches. Since the days of the Crusades Europeans had been acquainted with the goods of the Orient, silks and fine textiles, porcelains and china, gems, perfumes, woods, and most of all, spices. Crusaders had brought back samples from the Levant. Quickly Europeans wanted more.

During subsequent medieval years the Italians had served as middlemen, picking up these goods in depots of the Eastern Mediterranean and bringing their cargoes back to the home peninsula for distribution throughout Europe. For their service the Italian merchants demanded and collected most rewarding income, which served to build their cities and to support their gracious medieval living.

During the fourteenth century another factor entered the picture, the rising power of the unfriendly Ottoman Turks in the Eastern Mediterranean. After they captured Constantinople midway through the fifteenth century, the goods from the East reaching Europe became almost prohibitively expensive. This was serious, since many of those Eastern products which had started out as luxuries had grown into the category of necessities. This was particularly true of spices. The men of the West recognized that trade contacts must be maintained, and sought possible new routes.

Through much of the fifteenth century the Portuguese edged southward along the western coast of Africa, hoping to open a new route to the Indies by sea. They gained valuable experience in sailing the open ocean with the aid of new navigational instruments, such as the compass and the astrolabe, and with the design of stouter ships called caravels. In 1488, Bartholomeu Dias rounded the continent's southern tip. He was not equipped to follow through beyond the point which was appropriately titled the Cape of Good Hope. Eleven years later another Portuguese sea captain, Vasco de Gama, better prepared and provisioned, sailed beyond the Cape of Good Hope, reached Calicut beyond the Indian Ocean, and returned with the good news and, better still, a rich cargo from the Indies. Thus, as the fifteenth century closed, Portugal had a sea route to the East.

Meanwhile, however, another man had been dreaming, a Genoese who had been around the Iberian peninsula for some years past. Christopher Columbus had been reading and scheming and latterly arguing that, if the world was round, as many wise men of the day claimed, then it should be possible to reach the East by sailing across the mysterious Western Ocean. Even after Dias came back with his "good hope," Columbus was convinced that his projected westward route would be shorter and surer. However, he needed funds and a royal sponsor in order to test his *"Empresa de Indias"* (Enterprise of the Indies).

He tried the king of Portugal, and then the *reyes católicos*. Ferdinand of Aragon and Isabella of Castile. Isabella had been intrigued, but advisers were dubious and opposed. Finally, after the fall of Granada, the last step in the reconquest of Spain from the Moors, Isabella gave Columbus the required royal backing. Several courtiers had to furnish the funds, since Isabella's finances were badly depleted after she pawned the crown jewels to finance this "last crusade." With the equivalent of around eight thousand dollars Columbus secured three small ships, hired crews of adventuresome men, and headed westward into the unknown.

After event-filled weeks on the uncharted Western Ocean, ninety grateful men, on October 12, 1492, found dry land on the beach of Guanahani (Watling's Island).

Recognizing that their windfall was simply a small island, the white men sailed southward, saw Cuba, and then landed on an island which, because its landscape reminded them of home, they called Española (Hispaniola), modernly shared by the Republic of

Haiti and the Dominican Republic. The flagship, *Santa María,* had run aground on landing. As a result when Columbus turned back to report, early in 1493, some forty men had to remain behind in the little settlement of Navidad on the island.

The Spanish monarchs were enthusiastic over the news of the landfall and just as eagerly accepted the surmise of Columbus that the Asiatic mainland lay no great distance beyond the islands he had seen. They immediately asked the pope to confirm the claims which Columbus had made in the name of Castile. Alexander VI did that with his Line of Demarcation. When Portugal, fearing that the Spanish-born pope may have been overly generous, objected strenuously in 1494, the two powers agreed to move the international property line farther west by the Treaty of Tordesillas—all lands to the east were to be the sphere of Portugal, those to the west the area in which Spain might operate.

Determined to reinforce paper claims by actual occupation, Isabella ordered a fleet to be readied, with colonists, tools, provisions, seeds, domesticated animals and other trappings of civilization. Later in 1493 Columbus, now bearing the title "Admiral of the Ocean Sea," guided a fleet of seventeen ships back to Española, to make it a way station on the road to supposedly nearby Asia.

● **Spanish Dismay and Disillusionment**

The next years in Española were troubled. The colonists proved restless and unmanageable, and Columbus an inept administrator. He was replaced in 1502 by a royal governor, Nicolás de Ovando. Before too many more years it became painfully evident that the admiral had not reached the Indies of the East, or even lands lying off the shores thereof. Each westbound, northbound, southbound probe showed that instead he had run into not simply one but two giant landmasses, blocking Spanish access to the Orient.

Worse still, in 1513 Vasco Núñez de Balboa pushed out from the recent settlement of Darien on the Isthmus to find a whole new ocean beyond. Ten years later the men of Ferdinand Magellan came back to Spain to tell how great and vast Balboa's *Mar del Sur* actually was. These men did prove that Columbus was right; one could reach the East by sailing west, but the way was prohibitively long and dangerous, and for trade purposes impractical.

Meanwhile, the Portuguese seemed to be the lucky ones. Their trading empire in Calicut and the Spice Islands of the East Indies was booming. Lisbon was rapidly growing into *the* distributing center for all of Europe, as the riches of the East came back round the tip of Africa. Spanish dreams of great wealth were fading.

● Mexico: The First American "Jackpot"

In 1517 a band of adventurers under Fernández de Córdoba set out from Cuba to do a bit of slave-hunting in the islands to the north, this being currently the most rewarding enterprise, since Cuba had proved disappointing in treasure yield. Instead of heading north from Havana into the Lucayas (the Bahama island chain), this band decided to try their luck to the west. On the Yucatán peninsula they found natives clothed in woven cotton garments and whose cities could be seen rising inland. They were obviously peoples more advanced than any seen to date. When the Spaniards landed, however, these Indians, the great Maya, proved unpleasantly inhospitable. The white men, most of them badly wounded, took to their ships and turned back to Cuba to report their experience.

The next year Governor Diego de Velásquez dispatched Juan de Grijalva and a small company to gather further information. The Mayan reception had not changed in its fierce resistance, but, even so, Grijalva could confirm the report that they were culturally advanced. He decided to explore further. Rounding the Yucatán peninsula he crossed the Bay of Campeche and came to the shore of Tabasco. The Tabascans received the visitors cordially and offered golden presents, but begged the strange white men to return to the east from which they came—later the Spaniards learned that all this had been by the order of the Aztec emperor who, through fast runners, was kept informed of the doings of the white visitors. Among the Tabascans the Spaniards seem to have first heard of the great kingdom inland. Grijalva sent this last bit of information and much of the gold back to Cuba and continued to sail northward. His uncle, Governor Diego de Velásquez, was thrilled by the news and hurried to make preparations for the conquest of that inland empire. He chose Hernán Cortés as his lieutenant, but soon had second thoughts about his loyalty and summoned him to Havana for a conference.

Cortés had been in the Indies since 1504. He had gained notice in Española, had participated in the conquest of Cuba, had subsequently quarreled with Velásquez, but then the two had been reconciled. As of 1518 Cortés was the *alcalde* (mayor or ranking local official) of the southeastern town of Santiago. Immediately after appointment Cortés set to work to gather investors, to enlist some five hundred fortune seekers, and to ready eleven ships. The call to Havana roused his suspicions, and he decided to defy the governor's order. Instead, early in 1519 he sailed out of Santiago, completing the outfitting of his little flotilla as he proceeded. Thus, as he set out on his adventure, he was technically an outlaw—this fact is important in the sequel.

The little runaway fleet sailed along the coast of Maya-land and made for Tabasco. Contrary to what Grijalva had known, the newest white visitors were met with stout opposition. The Spaniards emerged victorious and in several important ways wiser. They found the great advantage which their firearms and cold steel gave them against a vastly superior Indian force, unacquainted with such weapons. Further, they recognized that their horses were terrifying allies against men who knew no such animals. They got little gold but did receive something destined to be even more valuable, namely, the Indian maid soon to be baptized Doña Marina. One of twenty female slaves given as a peace offering, Marina became not only Cortés' lady and mother of his son and heir, but also the second link in his interpreter chain. The Spaniards had already picked up shipwrecked Jerónimo de Aguilar, who spoke Maya, on the island of Cozumel. Now with Marina, Nahua-born and fluent in Maya from the days of her captivity, the Spaniards would be able to communicate with the Nahua-speaking Mexicans.

From Tabasco, Cortés sailed on to establish a coastal base and town at Villa Rica de la Vera Cruz founded on Good Friday. To this town ambassadors from the Aztec emperor in the highland came with gifts and the fervent entreaty that the white visitors return whence they came. Moctezuma, fully apprized of their movements, was deeply concerned, fearing that they might be emissaries of the god Quetzalcoatl, principal diety of the Aztec religion, or that their leader might even be the god himself, come back to fulfill an earlier prophecy of retribution for wrongs committed. The Spaniards were awed by the magnificence of the gold and silver offerings. Their appetites were whetted, their determination made firmer.

Cortés gathered information along the coast concerning the empire inland. He was delighted to learn that it was largely held together by force and fear and was in that measure vulnerable. The subject peoples thoroughly hated their imperial masters. He was told that only the fierce men of Tlaxcala had remained unconquered. Each passing day made Cortés more determined to advance. However, before he dared do this, there were two things to be done. He summoned his men and bade them, in proper Spanish fashion, to elect a town council, a *cabildo*, for Vera Cruz. Then to that legal body he resigned his command in order to receive it back as a legal appointment—he was looking ahead to be able to deal with his own emperor as, at least, a quasi-legitimate agent. Next, knowing that there was still a sizable pro-Velásquez faction among his men, he burned his ships to prevent desertion.

In August all was in readiness and the ascent of the *sierra* (mountains) began. The Spaniards battled and won the respect of the hold-out Tlaxcalans, who then joined forces with them. The little army survived, with the help of a tip-off by Marina, the Moctezuma-ordered ambush at Cholula. Next, the open-mouthed Spaniards were looking down from the heights on Tenochtitlán, the Aztec capital, set like a sparkling gem on its island in Lake Texcoco. Indecisive Moctezuma made yet another blunder and received the brash invaders into his imperial city in November 1519. He was quickly their captive.

The Spaniards sustained a temporary setback in mid-1520. Cortés had to hurry down to the coast to parry the threat of Pánfilo de Narváez, sent with a force by Velásquez to arrest him and to take charge in the name of the governor. Don Hernán was successful; he defeated Narváez, took him prisoner, and climbed back to the Valley of Mexico with several hundred new recruits. However, during his absence his deputy, impetuous Pedro de Alvarado had handled the Aztecs of the capital badly. Cortés found them in surly mood. When the Aztecs refused to listen to Moctezuma, bid by Cortés to remonstrate with them, and when during the emperor's speech a particularly angry native mortally wounded the "King of Men" with a thrown tile, Cortés recognized that he and his men were in deep trouble. The selection of fiery young prince Cuauhtémoc as the new Aztec leader further confirmed Cortés' apprehension. The Spaniards recognized the precariousness of their position. Cortés ordered a strategic withdrawal, at least for the moment. The Aztecs were alert and turned the dark hours of June

30 (1520) into *la noche triste* (sad night), slaughtering many of the invaders on the causeway, capturing others to be sacrificed to their gods, and sending much of the accumulated plunder to the bottom of the lake, lost by the Spaniards forever.

The next year the Spaniards fought back, with the aid of their loyal allies, the Tlaxcalans. Before May was gone, they were again in control. Soon the lieutenants of Cortés were fanning out far and wide, from the capital now renamed Ciudad de México, hoping to find other Indian kingdoms to rival the Aztec prize.

● **The Inca Empire of the Andes**

The exploits of Francisco Pizarro, Diego de Almagro, and another several hundred brash and courageous adventurers in the central Andes during the 1530s gave Spain a second reason to revise feelings about the American landfall of 1492. The Inca empire, of which Balboa had heard but did not live to conquer, was taken quite as dramatically as Mexico, but much more brutally. The two leaders were men of lowly origin in Spain and in the New World had hardly benefited by their training in Panama under the less than kindly Governor Pedro Árias de Ávila (Pedrarias). Too often these conquistadores, "nobodies" at home and suddenly become "somebodies" in the New World, sadly showed the lack of background to act the part of minor noblemen, called *hidalgos*, whom they fancied themselves to be.

In 1524 Pedrarias sanctioned the partnership of Pizarro and Almagro and gave them permission to go south in search of the rumored kingdom. A new governor at Panama, Pedro de los Rios, ordered Pizarro and his men to return. Pizarro determined to go over his head, to the king himself. He returned from Spain in 1530 with a royal patent for the conquest, with titles and many privileges, and from Almagro's point of view, too many Pizarro relatives to share the glory and the spoils. The rift between the two leaders began at that date. Internal rivalry was to be a constant in the early history of Spanish relations with Peru.

The expedition of conquest went south in 1531, and before that year was out Pizarro had confronted Emperor Atahualpa the Inca at Cajamarca and taken the native lord prisoner, emulating the earlier tactics of Cortés. Bit by bit the Spaniards spread through the leaderless empire, gathering its treasure, profaning its sacred cities, taking its capital, Cuzco, and subjugating its people. Atahualpa, the royal kidnapee, shrewdly saw their passion for gold and silver and proposed a fabulous ransom for his freedom, namely, to fill his prison room with such riches. The Spaniards agreed and marveled as the room was piled high with treasure— the ransom has been variously estimated from ten to forty million dollars. Whatever the total, the division of the loot turned all the members of the expedition into rich men, but far from sated their greed. In the end all the gold did Atahualpa no good. Pizarro found reason to put him to death, knowing well that his freedom would be fatal to the Spaniards.

On the Day of the Kings in 1535 (January 6), the conquistadores paused long enough to dedicate their new capital. Lima, *Ciudad de los Reyes* (City of Kings), was located some miles upland from the port of Callao, better placed for their purposes than distant Cuzco, far inland and high in the Andes.

Later in that same year (1535) Almagro went off to investigate Nuevo Toledo, his royally granted principality to the south. He returned thoroughly disillusioned with the land of Chile and definitely determined that Cuzco at least would be part of his jurisdiction. The Pizarros disagreed, and civil war ensued. Almagro lost his life in the fight, but his son, known as Almagro el Mozo, carried on the contest. He, too, was taken and executed, but not until his "Men of Chile" had surprised and killed Francisco Pizarro. The other Pizarros continued their bullying tactics, against Spaniards and Indians alike. One of them, Gonzalo, even chose to battle the king's newly appointed viceroy for control. It was close to mid-century before Peru was firmly under royal rule, in the days of the capable Pedro de la Gasca.

Earlier Francisco Pizarro's lieutenants had spread out along the Andean cordillera. Sebastián Benalcázar turned the old kingdom of Quito, modern Ecuador, into a Spanish province, before pushing farther north to carve out a principality for himself in Popayán, in modern Colombia.

The deaths of the Almagros, father and son, left the land to the south unclaimed. Pedro de Valdivia, in 1540, asked for and obtained Pizarro's permission to embark on the conquest of this province of Chile. He and his men went south, fully aware that Chile was not likely to be a land of quick and easy wealth, but determined to build another sort of prosperity, with the labor of the reportedly numerous Indians; theirs would be an agricultural province. They set their capital, Santiago, in the fertile valley of Chile. Thence they sought to expand southward but in the process ran into the toughest and most resourceful of Indian opponents, the Araucanians. These fierce natives, fighting desperately to hold onto their lands, turned southern Chile into a dangerous frontier. In their own way these Araucanians helped to form the Chileans into a hardy, alert, hardworking version of the colonial Spaniard, a breed not always matched elsewhere in the Spanish overseas empire.

Out of Peru the Spaniards also spread eastward, up the cordillera and onto the *altiplano* (plateau) of the future Bolivia, a province known in colonial times as Upper Peru. Here in the middle 1540s they found the fabulous Potosí, that veritable "mountain of silver." Within a few years this far-off boom town saw its population grow into six figures and its treasure yield into millions of pesos. Upper Peru was a mining province par excellence.

● Along the Spanish Mainland

The Spaniards originally called the northern shore of the southern continent *Tierra Firme*. Several men had sailed along its coast quite early. Then pearl fishers appeared along the eastern Venezuelan shoreline and on the island of Margarita. In general these exploiters treated the natives so harshly that even attempts by kindly missionaries to overcome the hate were fruitless. Farther west along the shoreline in the 1520s the Spaniards began to establish the first towns, such as Coro, but King Charles Hapsburg heavily in debt, turned over to German creditors all settlement and exploitation rights in this land of Venezuela. In 1530 the German banking house of the Welsers came into possession of this concession. The Germans failed to find El Dorado or the Land of Omagua or other rumored rich centers inland, but they did give ample proof that the Spaniards had no real or imputed monopoly on such unpleasant human acts as greed, rapacity, cruelty. The Germans handled both Indians and Spaniards equally shamelessly. Neither group wept when shortly before mid-century King Charles Hapsburg rescinded the Welser patent and allowed the Spaniards to come back to build the province.

To the west, in the province known as the kingdom of Nueva Granada, the modern Colombia, the Spaniards began coastal foundations early, Santa Marta being the first, in 1525, followed in 1533 by Cartagena. Then in 1536 they pushed upland into the interior to conquer the developing empire of the Chibchas. Gonzalo Jiménez de Quesada was the driving force, and although never able to lay hand on the accumulated treasures of these Chibchas, he kept the conquest quite humane. The presence of the Dominican friars, the White Robes, helped to make it so, and the Indians were rather quickly integrated into the Spanish society developing in such centers as Bogotá, the capital, Antioquia, Medellín, and Cali on parallel ribs of the cordillera. In time Nueva Granada rewarded the Spaniards with the yield of rich gold mines, and its abundant emeralds furnished still another source of wealth. The major seaport, Cartagena, long continued an important link in the Spanish trade system and a key bastion of Caribbean defense.

● The Atlantic Side of South America

Much of the Atlantic side of the southern continent Spain had to share with Portugal. By the Treaty of Tordesillas of 1494 Portugal had a rightful claim to the so-called "bulge of Brazil," the lands lying to the east of a north-south line extending, roughly, from the mouth of the Amazon to a point somewhat inland from the modern city of São Paulo.

In the 1530s, with the spectacular yield of its trading empire in the East declining, Portugal thought it opportune to pay some attention to its American claims. The crown-instigated survey of Affonso de Souza recommended instant action, lest alarmingly numerous French loggers negate the Portuguese claims *in fact,* though not perhaps in theory. Accordingly, the Portuguese crown made a series of so-called captaincy grants to wealthy men of the realm, hoping that these *donatarios* would be inclined to invest privately in their lands and, with a minimum expense to the royal treasury, lay the basis for a strong colony.

A dozen or so disappointing years of the experiment showed only two or three *donatarios* interested or resourceful enough to bring the royal hope to reality. Only royal financing and effort could ensure a strong Portuguese Brazil. Accordingly, in 1549 Tomé de Souza was named as royal governor of the captaincy of São Salvador (Bahía). To further show the seriousness of intent, the crown in that same year sent a contingent of Jesuits under Padre Manuel de Nobrega to begin missions among the Indians. Successive governors extended royal control. One of them, Mem de Sá, had to fend off a French colonization attempt at Rio de Janeiro. Portuguese colonists arrived and opened some of the agricultural potential of the territory, founding new cities, such as São Paulo, Belém, and Pernambuco. By 1580 two trends important for the future of Brazil were developing: the shift to sugar-growing as the prime agricultural effort and the beginnings of the introduction of African slaves as the chief element of the labor force, the Indians having been found quite untrainable and almost everywhere recalcitrant.

Initial Spanish interest in the Atlantic side of South America grew out of the hope that, perhaps, the rumored kingdom of the Incas might be reached via the network of rivers emptying into the ocean at the Río de la Plata estuary.

Even after Pizarro had reached the land of the Incas from the Pacific side, other Spaniards continued in the river provinces, hopeful that more rich kingdoms awaited discovery. The followers of Pedro de Mendoza in the 1530s explored widely. Then, under Domingo Martínez de Irala, they established a base far inland at Asunción. They pushed out into the Tucumán, where they soon met other Spaniards coming down from Upper Peru. On the eastern slopes of the Andes they ran into colonists from Chile crossing into the province of Cuyo. Gradually they worked down the Paraná to the estuary where finally in 1580 they succeeded in founding a Buenos Aires which was strong enough to repel the attacks of the fierce Charrúa Indians who had defeated several earlier attempts.

These river and plains provinces of the Atlantic southern side of the continent had little mineral wealth to offer. Spain held them but treated them somewhat as stepchildren, little interested in the products of their forests or the cattle of their plains.

● **The Explorers**

The discovery of rich Indian empires sparked the hope that other fairylands were waiting to be found and plundered. A generation of explorers followed that of the conquistadores. A fourth "G," for gullibility, was added to the more regular "Three Gs" (gold, glory, gospel). Once they had seen Mexico and Peru, the Spaniards were willing and anxious to believe fairytales could come true. And the Indians were coyly certain that what the Spaniards sought was just a little farther on—*"poco mas allá."*

Bimini and the Fountain of Youth drew Juan Ponce de León into Florida. When Pánfilo de Narváez got to the Land of Apalachee, he found it thoroughly disappointing. Like disappointment in large quantities was the lot of Hernando de Soto and his men as they ranged through the southeastern quadrant of the continent; the Mississippi was a great river but its waters were just plain muddy. No Isle of the Amazons was waiting for Nuño de Guzmán along Mexico's western coast. The adobe pueblos of the Zuñi Indians of New Mexico fell far short of fulfilling the dream of the Seven Golden Cities, and the reputed golden streets of Quivira proved very ungolden to Vásquez de Coronado and his men after they trekked far out onto the plains. The rosiest of hopes sent these starry-eyed Spaniards paining through burning deserts, scrambling over high and forbidding mountains, panting into dank jungles, sailing down great and treacherous rivers, facing almost unbelievable dangers, but fairytales did not come true. Even so, the explorers performed one valuable service: they furnished their fellow Spaniards with a wealth of geographic knowledge of the lands where they would build their empire.

3

Challenge, Consolidation, Expansion

● Challenge to Iberian Monopoly of the New World

Spain had established priority claim to the Americas by the fact of the Columbus discovery. In the earliest American years the other powers of Europe were too preoccupied with their own affairs to pay more than passing attention to developments across the Atlantic. Delighted by the first news from Mexico, Spain determined to keep her good fortune a secret, but the news soon spread. In the next years the seas closer home were alive with adventurers now as much intent on taking Spanish galleons returning from the Indies, as they had formerly been on intercepting Portuguese caravels laboring home from the East. Even after some pirate raids the books of the *Casa de Contratación* (Board of Trade) showed millions reaching Spain from the New World. To counteract this hijacking operation Spain developed the so-called *flota* system of annual fleets. Treasure ships assembled at Havana and the "silver fleet" proceeded homebound under convoy furnished by heavily armed warships. In an attempt to keep American waters clear of raiders, Spain also developed the *armada de barlovento,* a coast guard of small and fast-moving vessels.

After mid-century France made two settlement attempts, a "France Antarctica" in Brazil at the site of the future Rio de Janeiro in the 1550s and a bit later a Huguenot colony of refuge first in the Carolinas and then on the northern Florida coast. The Portuguese ousted the trespassing Frenchmen from Brazil. Spain quite unceremoniously routed the Gallic invaders from Florida and countered with the occupation of the peninsula—St. Augustine, founded in 1565, was the first enduring settlement within the

boundaries of the future United States. By this time France was
much too busy with civil war, her Wars of Religion, to press the
challenge in the Americas.

In the 1560s a group of ambitious English merchants sent John
Hawkins to the Spanish Indies with a small but well-stocked fleet.
The dual purpose was to test how seriously the Spanish colonials
took the royal prohibitions against trade with foreigners and, even
more, how badly these same colonials needed goods at prices com-
petitive with those exacted by the royal monopolists, the Seville
merchants. Encouraged by the "under-the-counter" business he
was able to do at Santo Domingo in 1563, Hawkins next tried
Tierra Firme in 1565. Having fared well enough, even though he
had to break down colonial reluctance, lately stiffened by royal
reiteration of the no-trade-with-foreigners policy, he was back in
the Caribbean in 1568 with a fleet of six ships, two of which
actually belonged to Queen Elizabeth herself. This time Hawkins
met much frightened sales resistance.

During the next decades Spain, which under Philip II became
the threatening symbol of a militant Catholicism, was at war with
such nations as had chosen the Protestant position in the theo-
logical and dynastic battle underway. The combination of anti-
Spanish forces became an "embattled Protestantism," in days
when religion and nationalism often fused into one—for example,
Catholic Spain, Protestant England.

Francis Drake became something of a symbol for the age and
with his daring deeds on both sides of the Atlantic set a pattern for
"singeing the beard of the king of Spain." In 1570 he surprised the
royal treasure house at Nombre de Dios and then hijacked the
silver packtrain from Peru as it crossed the Isthmus of Panama. He
and others were several times back in the Caribbean, terrorizing
and sacking. In the late 1570s he slipped through the Strait of
Magellan into the Pacific to harass the Spaniards and then continued on around the world, so as not to face retaliation in American waters on a homebound return along the way he had come.
The Dutch who had recently won their freedom from Spain in a
brutal and bloody struggle joined in the fray. Spain's ally Portugal
was their main target, at home, along the African coast, and in
the Indies of the East. In 1588 in this continuing war Spain suffered a serious and crippling setback, when the "Invincible
Armada," dispatched by Philip II to punish the Dutch and the
English, was defeated in the famous encounter in the Downs of the

English Channel. This was a hard but not a mortal blow. It did, however, mark an end to Spain's supremacy on the seas and within a few years made it possible for her rivals to challenge the American monopoly more effectively with the establishment of actual American colonial empires.

In the seventeenth century the English dug in at Virginia and in New England, and a little later planted a colony in Maryland. The French settled in the Saint Lawrence Valley and began to edge westward. The Dutch were temporarily on the Hudson, and the Swedes on the Delaware. English, French, and Dutch picked up unoccupied islands in the Lesser Antilles, and for a quarter of a century the Dutch seized and held the "sugar-coated" tip of Brazil. Spain's protests were cavalierly ignored, and she could do little to oust the interlopers.

● **Consolidation and Expansion to 1700**

The century and a half from mid-sixteenth through the end of the seventeenth is of considerable importance in the history of Latin America. The Age of the Conquistadores had ended about 1550. The great native empires had been won and most of the rumors concerning others had been run down and proven false. The Spaniards' view of the future had sobered greatly. Nearly all recognized that the days of quick and easy wealth had passed. They and their fellows had most probably scooped up the bulk of the treasure which the Indians had accumulated during the ages. But it really was not the end, for the later 1540s had shown some of the sources on which the Indians had drawn. There was Potosí in Upper Peru and the mine strike in Zacatecas in Mexico, both rich in silver. There had to be more, but the problem would be to find these. Less exciting and much more prosaic days were ahead— hopefully, however, as rewarding and prosperous, even though they would be so at the price of hard work. This prospect really did not seriously bother the Spaniards, since they knew that they would not have to do that work. Their Indies had a great potential work force in the thousands of Indians, their new subjects. And even if this force wasted away, as was already happening in the islands, the Spaniards were confident that they would have the means to import labor from Africa.

Consolidation of what had already been won must be a first step. This meant the establishment in the new lands of a sound and working American version of Old World society. Much of this story will be studied in the next chapter, when institutional life will be the theme. Along with this consolidation went what might be termed supportive expansion, to open new opportunities. The search for mines and the establishment of missions were the chief keys but other forces, too, were at work.

In Peru, after overrunning the Inca empire and taking the Indian capital of Cuzco, the Spaniards recognized a serious problem. Cuzco, set high in the mountains, may have been ideal for the Incas but its difficult accessibility from the sea was a handicap. The sea was the Spaniards' link with Europe and their homeland. Accordingly, they early built a new capital, Lima, within easy distance of the port of Callao, and developed other towns along the coast. Lima was very much a Spanish city transplanted to the New World, magnificent in its richness, with its spacious plaza and parks, its fine streets, its great public buildings, its many churches and monasteries, its stately homes, its university. Long the capital, not only of Peru, but of all South America, it became a gaudy model for other centers. Its population was heavily European, although it had its Indian slums or *barrios*.

Mining dominated the economy of Peru and its daughter province on the *altiplano* (plateau), Upper Peru. Both had to count heavily on neighbors for foodstuffs and on the mother country for their manufactured needs. Not gold-silver rich, colonial Chile was one of the more successful of Spain's agricultural provinces. Its climate was temperate, its soil fertile, its Indians numerous, and its Spaniards content to be modern versions of the great medieval landed barons. Across the cordillera in the plains-river provinces of future Argentina the situation was quite similar, with the exception that there cattle were more important than foodstuffs. The great wheat-growing days on the *pampa* were still well into the future nineteenth century.

In the mountain provinces prospectors and miners generally led the way. The missionaries came a bit later and were expected to be the principal agents of not only Christianization but also Hispanicization. The Spaniards wanted Christian Indians but they were even more interested in peaceful Indians who could fit into the society which was developing. Often the settlers were more than a little irked by the efforts of the missionaries to protect their neophytes from the much too frequent demands for their labor.

One of the most successful, certainly the most publicized, of the mission efforts was that of the Jesuits in the so-called Reductions of Paraguay. In the Paraguay forests and on the upper reaches of the Río Paraná, the Black Robes, beginning in the early seventeenth century, set up a series of Indian towns into which they sought to attract their prospective converts. At the peak of their development a century later the reductions numbered thirty and served an estimated 150,000 Indians. The priests kept the towns isolated from contact and frequent bad example of the colonists. There they taught their charges not only Christian doctrine but also the ways and skills of the white man's civilization. The reductions became a mini-kingdom, in large measure economically self-sufficient. The expulsion of the Jesuits from the Spanish Indies in 1767 put an end to the experiment.

Northward on the Atlantic side was Portuguese Brazil. By the end of the sixteenth century sugar had definitely outdistanced the forest woods and lesser competitors, such as tobacco, for economic superiority in the colony. The plantations (*fazendas*) of the "bulge" provinces were many and profitable, the large majority still located along the littoral, within easy transportational reach of the ocean. Some ranchers did move inland and began to run cattle along the Río São Francisco and tributaries to help feed the growing population of the sugar provinces. Bahía and Pernambuco-Olinda remained populous and thriving towns. Far to the south was São Paulo. The area was in too chilly a climate to permit either sugar or cotton culture. The residents of the province or captaincy were known as Paulistas; they were active and enterprising and much interested in finding some stable basis for their economy. For a time these hardy *bandeirantes* thought to find an answer in slave-raiding into the interior, especially after they discovered the Jesuit missions on the upper Paraná with their ready-made supply of potential captives. This raiding continued until the padres obtained Spanish royal permission to arm and train their neophytes into a very effective militia. Then the Paulistas had to range elsewhere in the backcountry. During these forays in the later seventeenth century the Paulistas discovered the gold deposits of Minas Gerais, and a little later diamonds. In the eighteenth century mining activities worked a marked change in the colony's population and economic patterns. In more modern times the coffee culture has become a mainstay of southland economy.

In the north the Portuguese edged up the Amazon and carried on slaving among the jungle Indians and opened some small-scale exploitation of such tropical riches as woods, drugs, and American spices. An armed conflict with Spain midway through the next century ended with the Peace of 1750 which rubbed out the Tordesillas Line and gave Brazil approximately its modern boundary. A very important seventeenth-century development in Brazil was the wholesale introduction of African black slaves. The Portuguese were never able to turn their Indians into an effective labor force.

Spanish expansion from northern Peru, out of the kingdom of Quito (Ecuador), and beyond the areas of the Spanish Mainland's occupied centers was regularly across the cordillera (mountain range) and just as regularly a mission enterprise. Early mining prospecting there had shown little or nothing to attract exploiter attention. Franciscans and Jesuits went into the *montaña* or the *oriente,* as the eastern slope of the cordillera was called, in search of souls and laid the groundwork for the large province of Las Maynas. Jesuits went out of Bogotá to evangelize the natives of the Meta-Casanare region and other reaches of the upper Orinoco watershed. Farther east, on the *llanos* (plains) behind Caracas, Capuchins, a branch of the Franciscans, extended Spanish influence into interior Venezuela. Few civilians of the day followed the missionaries.

Through the Central American strip, the captaincy-general of Guatemala, the Spaniards did not have much room for expansion. The majority of the early towns were set on the Pacific side and in the highlands away from the debilitating heat of the coast. The natives had similar settlement patterns.

Activity in the Caribbean during the seventeenth century was carried on more often by Spain's rivals and competitors, intent on getting into the sugar-raising business. Here, midway through the century, Spain sustained her one major territorial loss, when in the days of Oliver Cromwell the English seized and held the formerly Spanish-occupied island of Jamaica. In that century this so-called American Mediterranean became most interestingly international, an area of fierce rivalries and almost constant jockeying, both by arms and in diplomacy. For a time it was the playground of the troublesome multinational buccaneers whose loyalties were as often to themselves as to a European power. So great a universal scourge did they become that late in the century all the European nations combined to eliminate them and put an end to their fearsome depredations.

● Mexico's Northward Movement

To this point most of the expansionist story has been sketched in general terms. A more detailed account of one such drive can show the varied elements involved. Chosen as reasonably typical is the northward expansion of New Spain during the seventeenth century.

Most historians of this northward movement beyond the confines of the recently conquered Aztec empire have seen it as a three-pronged advance. This, quite certainly, is a *post-factum* reading, not something definitely planned in advance, but it does nevertheless quite enlighteningly describe what actually happened between, roughly, 1550 and 1700 in Mexico. There was a central line of progression northward from the capital to the upper Rio Grande valley in New Mexico, between the two Sierra Madre ranges. The right flank pushed north from Pánuco toward the lower reaches of that same Rio Grande and put the Spaniards in a position for their eighteenth-century swing along the Gulf Coast into Texas. The left flank edged northward through the lands of the so-called western slope, the territory lying between the Sierra Madre Occidental and the Gulf of California, and put the Spaniards into Arizona, from whence later in the eighteenth century they would push the line of occupation into California.

As of 1543 hopes of finding "another Mexico" in the northern continent were pretty thoroughly dashed. Coronado and his men had come back empty-handed from Cíbola and Quivira in 1542. The next year the De Soto survivors came into Pánuco with matching tales of disappointment for lands to the east. And the Cabrillo-Ferrelo probe up the outside of the continent failed to turn up anything of promise. About the time the future in New Spain was taking on a very drab complexion, word came into the viceregal capital of the rich silver find at Zacatecas, in the nearer north. As of 1548 the Mexican northern movement got under way, with miners and prospectors in the vanguard. They were prominent in many advances.

Things happened rapidly. More rich silver lodes were uncovered in the next years—Aguascalientes, Guanajuato, Pachuca, and San Luis Potosí. Eager prospectors flocked north and mining camps quickly developed into towns. A new province, Nueva Vizcaya, was cut off from Nueva Galicia and put in charge of the energetic Francisco de Ibarra. Durango became the northern capital. To the

east Francisco de Urdiñola pushed past San Luis Potosí into southern Coahuila. In 1575 his son, of the same name, founded Saltillo and a few years later tried an interesting experiment by bringing a colony of Christian Tlaxcalan Indians north to anchor and stabilize this corner of the frontier. Farther to the east Luis de Carbajal, pushed north from Pánuco to lay the foundations of Nuevo León, where Monterrey became another northern capital. By this time the line of camps and towns of the middle advance had reached southern Chihuahua. The far left flank, along the western slope, was advancing more slowly as it edged north from Culiacán.

As the frontier moved beyond the sphere of civilizing influence of the Aztec empire, the Spaniards ran into a new kind of Indian, fiercer, wilder, and less inclined to submit to new masters. These Chichimecas and their seminomad fellows harassed the mining camps, raided supply and ore trains, and consistently refused to furnish the labor teams demanded. Franciscan friars, keeping pace with the advancing frontier, worked strenuously but had little success with this new brand of native. When Spanish officials, angry and desperate, talked of solving the Indian problem by extermination, the friars pleaded and won a reprieve for the troublemakers. The friars asked that the mission, with royal support and armed protection, be given a trial as the solution.

The Franciscans and the Jesuits, who had been standing by awaiting a call to the frontier, quite conclusively proved that the mission could be a reasonably humane solution to inevitable confrontation inherent in each advance. The mission was shown to be an institution for the conversion of the Indians and also for the transfer of Spanish ways and civilization. This lesson of northern Mexico had a marked effect in the expansionist drives elsewhere in Latin America—the mission became a prime institution on Spanish frontiers.

During the last decades of the sixteenth century the frontier line in New Spain was moving steadily northward, even though not always along an even front. For example, in the middle it had reached into southern Chihuahua, at Santa Bárbara. But on the Gulf of Mexico side it lagged. And on the Gulf of California side it was holding precariously in southern Sinaloa. Even so, an interesting set of circumstances in the 1580s prepared a thrust of the middle frontier well beyond the line of effective occupation to the upper reaches of the Rio Grande. The establishment of the New

Mexican salient showed two aspects of Spanish frontier expansion, mission interest and the aspect of defense against possible threat from a colonial rival, which later would be characteristic of Spanish advance in the eighteenth century.

In 1580 one of the friars of Santa Bárbara, Fray Agustín Rodríguez, applied for and received permission to go north to investigate the mission potential of this pueblo-land. The next year with two other friars and a small band of soldiers Rodríguez toured pueblo-land and saw its potential firsthand. When he and his friar companions chose to remain in the north, Franciscan brethren worried and the next year sent a rescue expedition north. This band, under Antonio de Espejo, found that the friars had been murdered but picked up rumors of rich mines. What they had to tell awakened interest not only on the frontier but also at the Court of Spain. The viceroy of New Spain was ordered to find a man, wealthy and willing, to carry through a conquest—to be done with private funds. Philip II hoped not only for a harvest of souls but also for new supplies of riches for the royal treasury.

The monarch seems to have had still another reason for this sudden interest in the far north. In the early 1580s news drifted into Spain of the recent exploits of Francis Drake. It was known that he had been in the Pacific, that after raiding several Mexican coastal towns, he had run the California shoreline and made claims for Queen Elizabeth. Also it was hinted that Drake had found the western outlet of the alleged transcontinental Strait of Anian. If this was true and if England were to exploit this shortcut to the Pacific, a determined enemy could be uncomfortably close to the developing silver provinces of northern Mexico. Hence, a far outpost might be a sound defensive move.

There were a number of applicants for the patent of conquest. Not until 1595 was a choice made, Juan de Oñate, scion of one of the prominent frontier and Zacatecas mining families. Oñate and his company, 129 soldier settlers, some with families, and ten Franciscans, moved north in 1598. The next years Oñate laid the foundations of the colony of New Mexico, cowed the Indians, explored widely but found no great wealth, proved himself an inadequate leader of disappointed and disgruntled settlers, and was finally replaced, in 1609, by a royal governor, Pedro de Peralta. A few years before there had been serious thought of abandoning the project altogether, but the lobbying of the Franciscans had changed the royal mind. New Mexico was retained because of the promise it seemed to give of large-scale conversions. However, this Franciscan dream was never fully realized.

For a dozen years in the later seventeenth century (1680–) the Pueblos in revolt took back their homeland but could not withstand the reconquest effort of Don Diego de Vargas in the 1690s. By the end of the century the Spaniards were again secure on the upper Rio Grande.

They never succeeded in closing the territorial gap between the north Mexican provinces and New Mexico. The little knot of towns and missions in the El Paso district, most of them founded by the refugees from the Pueblo Revolt of 1680, did not expand beyond a way station between Parral and Chihuahua to the south and Socorro, the first of the Pueblo towns, in the north. Even so, in the eighteenth century New Mexico served well as a bulwark against marauding Indians from the mountains and the plains and as a deterrent to French advance from the Mississippi Valley.

Northward expansion on the east or Gulf of Mexico flank was long stalled by unfriendly Indians. Both Coahuila and Nuevo León were slow in developing. However, by the end of the seventeenth century the Franciscans had strategic missions on the Rio Grande, one of which, San Juan Bautista, would serve as gateway to Texas in the defensive move of the next century.

On the left or Gulf of California flank, along the western slope of the Sierra Madre, progress was steady through the seventeenth century. This was Jesuit land and a fine example of the mission frontier in action. The Black Robes arrived on the Rio Sinaloa in 1591. Thence they moved to the valleys of the Fuerte and the Mayo and the Yaqui. This last river was a network of many streams originating back in the Sierra. The Jesuits followed these systematically and had great success with the Ópata, who became exemplary as Christians and as Hispanicized natives.

From the Yaqui network the Jesuits crossed the watershed into the valley of the Sonora and its tributaries, ultimately into the Pimería Alta. In 1687 the "apostle of the Pimería" arrived on the scene, the remarkable Eusebio Francisco Kino. From his home base on the Rio San Miguel, Kino extended the frontier to the valley of the Rio Altar and then crossed the next watershed into the future Arizona. His foundation at San Xavier del Bac, on the northward-flowing Santa Cruz, put the frontier in a position to move on toward the Gila. Besides his work as apostle, Kino taught his converts the techniques of stock raising and more sophisticated agriculture. He was also an explorer and cartographer. In his ranging outward Kino came up with the proof that the California land across the Gulf was a peninsula, not an island, as had been thought since the early seventeenth century.

This discovery led him to encourage his fellow Italian, Padre Juan María Salvatierra, to make a new attempt to missionize Baja California. He dreamed of the day when a chain of Jesuit missions running up the peninsula might join with those of Pimería Alta at the Rio Colorado and then go on to Sebastián Vizcaíno's "great harbor of Monterey." The realization of this dream was still sixty years into the future.

As the mission frontiers in northern Mexico spread out, the lands behind were ready for the coming of the *paisanos*. Once the Indians were under control, life for the miners and the prospectors, farmers and ranchers, merchants and traders became reasonably safe and the civilian frontier, too, moved northward. Spain was occupying and colonizing its empire, not simply "conquering" and exploring the lands.

This story was repeated on many of the frontiers of the southern continent. Miner, missionary, and soldier were the key figures of Spanish expansion everywhere in the Americas, and the mission a very effective institution of both Christianization and Hispanicization.

4

Colonial Rule and Society

Even though Columbus in 1493 brought back no real evidence that he had reached the Indies of the East, the monarchs of Spain were willing to share his conviction that the islands seen lay close to the rich goal which he sought. Isabella of Castile immediately determined to occupy Española as the first step in building a Spanish empire overseas. In time Columbus' report was proved geographically incorrect, but the early royal moves were to affect the future of much of the two uncovered continents. The institutional life of the future Latin America began in 1493.

● **Conquerors and Conquered**

The Portuguese of the fifteenth century, as they inched down the African coast in search of a route to the Indies, had set an unfortunate precedent. First they brought back the material riches of the lands they touched; next they brought back the natives of those lands to be sold as slaves. Following that example, the several natives whom Columbus brought back were meant to be samples of Spain's new subjects and then be sold as slaves. Queen Isabella, however, would not sanction such a sequel and immediately declared the people of her new lands her free vassals, thereby conferring on them equal status with the common peasants of Castile. She was not opposed to their becoming workers for wages, as other Spanish free men. But despite this ruling the first Spaniards in Española treated the natives as slaves.

When Nicolás de Ovando arrived in Española as Isabella's agent, he had strict instructions to put an end to this Indian slavery. Ovando acted immediately, but just as quickly almost all work on the island came to a halt—fields went untilled, mines were not worked, roads were not laid, building came to a standstill. The new colonists, no matter how lowly or servile their status at home, considered that the ocean crossing had raised them to rank of "gentlemen" or *hidalgos*. Traditionally it was beneath the dignity of such *hidalgos* to work, since that was the function of the lower class. Instead they consigned the people they had conquered to this category. When the Indians, freed by Ovando's order, not only did not answer the help-wanted signs, but even moved into the interior, the situation became critical. A solution was imperative.

Playing on the queen's well-known desire to see her new subjects Christianized, the colonists argued that, unless contact were maintained, this pious aim was unrealizable. They argued that keeping the Indians close would best enable their conversion and, besides, would ensure the necessary labor force. Isabella yielded, with multiple conditions, such as paying the Indian workers just wages. The crown thus sanctioned the relationship between conqueror and conquered, by making forced labor the basic pattern.

Two institutions, already tried during the recent Spanish conquest of the Canary Islands, the *repartimiento* and the *encomienda*, were introduced to regularize these relationships. The *repartimiento* was a system by which the Indians were parceled out by a royal official to do a specific job. The period of service was limited, wages were to be paid, and calls for labor were to be spaced. The Indian, however, did not enjoy the option of working or not working; he worked whether he liked it or not. In parts of the future empire, this system was also known as the *mita*. In the *encomienda,* much more feudal in character, a group of Indians was assigned or "commended" to a Spaniard by way of reward for services rendered to the crown. The *encomendero* was to be the protector of his Indians and was to look to their conversion, and in return he was to be paid the tribute owed to the crown by all citizens, including the Indians. In theory both parties benefited, but in practice the system was open to serious abuses, particularly when the Indian, unable to pay the specified tribute in gold or silver, found his obligation transmuted into service for the *encomendero*. Herein can be seen some of the roots of the Indians' future condition of peonage.

By these two institutions the American native was put into a situation of forced labor which was often only a thin legal line away from actual enslavement. Though by law the native was always a free vassal of the crown, his actual condition was little different from that of a slave. Monarchs consistently and by varied decrees and formal legislation, such as the Laws of Burgos of 1512 and 1513 and the New Laws of 1542, sought to protect the Indian, by limiting the demands which could be made of him, specifying the obligations of the *encomenderos* to the Indians, and establishing detailed regulations concerning the treatment of the Indians. Even so, the colonists several thousand miles away bypassed, thwarted, and at times openly flouted these humanitarian attempts at regulation. Some royal officials and more regularly churchmen fought to eliminate abuses and to preserve the human rights of the Indians.

Most famous in the churchman group was the Dominican friar and bishop of Chiapas, Bartolomé de Las Casas, who spent much energy preaching, writing, arguing, and lobbying for the native Americans and in the process became a stellar champion of human rights. He had many emulators, such as the Franciscan Toribio de Motolinía, the Augustinian Alonso de la Vera Cruz, and the Mexican bishop Vasco de Quiroga. In 1537 Pope Paul III, in the bull *Sublimis Deus,* solemnly proclaimed that the Indians were human beings, children of God, and redeemed by Christ his son. This was designed to squelch the assertions of the exploiters that, since the Indians were of lesser breed and just a step removed from animals, they could be enslaved with a clear conscience.

These forced-labor institutions introduced into the islands were brought to the mainland by the conquistadores. The system worked tolerably well in the conquered Indian empires where traditions of labor and tribute had long prevailed. They broke down when frontiers advanced into areas where the natives had not been conditioned to work for and pay tribute to Indian overlords. In these areas the mission often was successful in regulating relations of conquerors and conquered. In time the *encomienda* was phased out, but the *repartimiento* and the *mita* continued through the colonial centuries.

The Portuguese initially tried similar forced-labor practices in Brazil. The Indians of Brazil, however, proved less tractable and adaptable. Before the end of the sixteenth century the Portuguese were solving their labor problem by the wholesale introduction of black slaves from Africa. It should be noted that the Spaniards, too, resorted to this expedient in areas where the native population declined almost to extinction or where the measures protecting the Indians were operative—in the island colonies, in tropical plantations, and in later mining operations.

● **Transfer of Things and Institutions**

With Columbus' second voyage (1493) the transfer of Old World material culture to the New began. Old World domesticated animals were imported early—cattle, hogs, sheep, goats, horses, mules, and donkeys. The Spaniards also brought Old World cereals and bread grains, up to that time unknown in the Americas, notably wheat, along with many vegetables, and new varieties of fruits, such as the citrus family, nuts, and spices. Importantly, they introduced the wheel, more efficient tools of iron and steel, and new skills and techniques. One of the Old World transplants, sugar cane, became extremely important and profitable in island colonies and in Brazil. In time sugar was a factor not only in economic life, but also in later international rivalries, especially in the Caribbean—no small amount of the Latin American story can be told with sugar as a central theme.

There was reciprocity from New World to Old as well. Most obvious of things moving from west to east were gold and silver. But there was also maize, new kinds of beans, members of the gourd family, the potato, tobacco, cacao, vanilla, chicle, highly useful drugs such as quinine and cocaine. Rubber, too, was a New World contribution.

Quite as quickly as material things, the colonizing powers introduced their institutions, political, social, economic, cultural, and their ways of living and working, enjoying themselves, expressing themselves, of thinking and praying. As conquerors, Spaniards and Portuguese were able to impose their ways and their ideas, with the result that the colonial Latin Americas showed a very definite European stamp.

● **The Concept of Royal Absolutism**

As Europe moved out of the Middle Ages into the sixteenth century, often reckoned as the beginning of the Modern Age, monarchs and princes acquired complete control not only over their lands but over their subjects as well. Absolutism was really not a new phenomenon, since it had been characteristic of many of the empires of ancient times. But then came the centuries of feudalism, when kings had to share power with strong nobles who could check, block, and even negate royal wishes and commands.

Late medieval developments, such as the emergence of the capitalist economy, the rise of the middle class, and the growth of nationalism, contrived to lessen the power of the landed nobility and to make it possible for princes to cut free from feudal obligations and restraints and centralize control, thereby strengthening their own personal power. This trend would become quite universal in Europe by the end of the sixteenth century, but in the early forefront were the kings of Spain, Ferdinand and Isabella, Charles the Fifth, and Philip II. These were the individuals who established the framework of the Spanish empire overseas. Absolutism, therefore, became a marked characteristic.

● Absolutism in Practice

The newly discovered lands overseas were considered to be the exclusive patrimony of the monarch in his role as king of Castile. He was supreme, from him came all authority, rights, and privilege. He made all appointments, issued all decrees, drafted all laws, and was the final source of all justice. Obviously, no matter how omnipotent he might be, it was not likely that he was likewise omnicompetent. He could not personally attend to all the details of his realm even at home and most certainly not abroad. He had to have helpers and/or agencies who, by delegated power, acted for him. In the Spanish colonial system these were many.

At home, in Spain, the absolute king was assisted by two powerful agencies. As early as 1502 the *Casa de Contratación* (House of Trade), was established in Seville to supervise the developing economic life overseas, trade and commerce, immigration, navigation, and in time the postal service. The *Casa* checked all persons and ships going to or returning from the Indies, and particularly all treasure returning home. Next, there was the Council of the Indies, established formally in the 1520s. This body was the real agent of colonial control. The councillors, very often men who had served in the Indies, framed the laws for royal signature, nominated officials to be appointed and later checked on their performance overseas, handled the royal budget for the colonies, administered the king's right of royal patronage over the colonial church and churchmen, served as a court of appeal from colonial tribunals or *audiencias*, and looked to most of the day-to-day tasks and functions of government. The king and the council kept in touch with developments overseas by much two-way correspondence and by periodic *visitadores*, sent out as inspectors or troubleshooters. A further check was provided by the so-called *residencia*, a stern review of performance to which each major retiring overseas officer was liable.

On the American side the roster of officers was much more complicated. In the early decades governors exercised royal authority or sometimes this was done by *audiencias*, small bodies of judges who had not only judicial but also administrative power. In the early days, too, the king on occasion appointed *adelantados*, men who were commissioned to conquer a region which they then ruled in his name. As the empire grew, so did the administrative structure. The Indies were divided into two large viceroyalties, that of New Spain in North America, with capital in Mexico City, and that of Peru for the other continent. Antonio de Mendoza who arrived in Mexico in 1535 was the first viceroy. The first of the viceroys of Peru had a rather difficult job in bringing dissident factions under control. Pedro de la Gasca in the late 1540s succeeded in firmly establishing royal control. Francisco de Toledo, seventh in the line who held office from 1569-81, did such a remarkable job that he is often called "the founder of Spanish rule in Peru."

The viceroy, as royal deputy and "the king's other self," was the ranking officer within his jurisdiction and ruled with the king's overall power. As captain-general he was responsible for colonial defense; as governor he supervised the Indians and was especially charged to see that laws protecting them were observed; he was watchdog of the royal treasury; he was president of the *audiencia* of his capital city, which gave him a measure of judicial power; finally, he served as vice-patron, looking after the king's rights in ecclesiastical affairs. The original term of the viceroy was indefinite, but in time it came to be three years; this made for a rapid turnover but prevented one man from becoming too powerful. The viceroys generally were of the nobility, and with very few exceptions were natives of Spain.

As the king needed helpers, so did the viceroy. There were captains-general and governors to rule the provinces, all royally appointed but immediately answerable to the viceroy. So, too, were the judges of the *audiencias* within the viceroyalty, the officers of the *Real Hacienda* (royal treasury), and lesser public officials.

The ranking local official was the *alcalde mayor* or, in Indian towns, the *corregidor,* responsible not only for the town but the district roundabout. These were appointed in most instances by the viceroy. In towns there were *alcaldes ordinarios* or justices, the *alguacil* or police chief, and the *alférez* or standard-bearer. There was, besides, a body of *regidores* who made up the *cabildo* or *ayuntamiento,* as the town council was known. In earlier times the *regidores* were elected by the citizenry, but gradually this elective process was eroded with the post of councilman going to the highest bidder or being held indefinitely by a person of influence. As is evident, the colonists had little or no part in shaping their political existence. Absolutism begat a stifling paternalism, and all the subject was expected to do was to obey.

Absolutism intruded into all aspects of colonial life. For example, the crown decided who might immigrate to the Indies, limiting the opportunity to its religiously orthodox subjects. From the first, Jews and Moors living in Spain were excluded. Later, after the breakup of religious unity in Europe, Spain was adamant in barring non-Roman Christians—for long years all dissident Christians were labeled *luteranos* and distinctly unwelcome. Portugal was somewhat less strict and intolerant on that score, just as Portuguese interpretations of absolutism were less unbending. Even so, both Spain and Portugal chose the Roman brand of Christianity as their state religion and accorded it exclusive favor in their American empires.

Royal absolutism governed policies and practice of trade and commerce. Understandable were regulations which would ensure that the mother country would benefit most from the wealth flowing from the colonies overseas, but sometimes rules and regulations seemed needlessly all-embracing and restrictive. Foreigners were forbidden to do business with or in the Indies. However, not even all Spaniards were allowed to participate. Very early the crown granted an exclusive trading monopoly to the Seville merchants, which was highly detrimental to the colonial buyer and seller. The crown refused to hear complaints.

Again, the better to ensure royal control, all export trade originated in strictly specified ports at home and could move only into equally specified ports in the Indies, and passage in both directions could only be at specified times and under royal convoy. For example, in the Indies, Santo Domingo in the islands, Nombre de Dios and later Portobelo on the Caribbean side of the Isthmus,

Cartagena on Tierra Firme, and Vera Cruz in Mexico were the only legitimate ports of entry. For the return to Spain, Havana (Cuba) was the final assembly station for all homebound traffic. On the Pacific side there was Acapulco in Mexico, Panama City on the Isthmus, Callao in Peru, and with certain restrictions Valparaiso in Chile. Not until late in the eighteenth century was Buenos Aires sanctioned as a legitimate port of entry and exit. Thus for long decades residents of the river-plains provinces were forced to receive their goods via the Isthmus, the port of Callao, and the lengthy haul over the mountains.

The system regularly put the colonists at a serious disadvantage and gave birth to a strong temptation to smuggling. Spain's colonial rivals, the English, the French, and preeminently the Dutch, were only too willing to profit by the situation. Spain could not be budged from the conviction that colonies existed, first, last, and always, for the exclusive benefit of the mother country and those subjects at home whom the crown chose to favor. Spain was far ahead in practice of seventeenth-century theorists who made such an attitude a key tenet of their mercantilist creed. Thus the colonies were not allowed to develop an economy of their own, but rather were compelled to serve as part of the economy of the mother country, by furnishing it with raw materials and needed goods, as well as serving as a protected market for home products. This was in addition to the colonial role as the source of the capital, in the form of gold and silver, that served as the means of building Spain into the world's richest and foremost power. The objective of the crown was the promotion of the power and standing of Spain, not the colonies, since these were simply a means to an end.

As though all this was not enough, the crown multiplied taxes and imposts. There were export and import levies, convoy exactions, the *alcabala* or sales tax, and many more. Besides the crown set up royal monopolies on many much used items, for example, mercury which became highly important in the reduction of silver ore. Wherever the colonist turned he found himself at the mercy of an ever-greedy crown. Again, interests in Spain were "protected" against colonial competition. For example, vine-planting and wine-making when not forbidden altogether were at very least severely restricted, as was the cultivation of the olive tree and the production of olive oil.

Latin American colonials enjoyed no more economic freedom than they did political self-determination.

● **The Makeup of Colonial Society**

In the Iberian peninsula, as in most of Europe, during the medieval centuries land was the chief determinant both of wealth and social status. Those who owned land were ranged at the top of the economic and also the social ladder—such men became known as nobles. Or one simply lived on the land and worked it for another—such men were peasants. In time a third class emerged which neither owned land nor worked it but whose contribution to society was in the form of service, as trader, merchant, craftsman, professional man—these were the bourgeoisie or middle class. This basic pattern for the organization of society came to the New World with the immigrants. Due to circumstances it was destined to be altered in some respects.

With almost unlimited land available to even the lowliest Spaniard or Portuguese, making possible a greatly expanded landowner class, land lost some of its magic as a narrowly shared blessing. All of the conquerors could be landowners. Since the nonowners regularly were the conquered, race quickly set off one class from the other, the white owners and the red nonowners. In time a third racial element, the African black, came in to broaden the racial spectrum. Therefore, Latin American colonial society was set up on the basis of race, with the conquering whites at the top.

Soon, however, even on the top there was a division, the Spaniards born in Spain became the *peninsulares* and those born in the colonies the *criollos*. After the passing of the generation of the conquistadores this became a definite reality. The *peninsulares* were almost exclusively the royal officials and their families, sent over to rule. They were never a majority but made up in arrogance what they lacked in numbers.

Quite early strong antipathy toward the *peninsulares* built among the *criollos*. These Americans were even more resentful toward the crown which had, as they saw it, arbitrarily ranked them as second-class citizens simply because of the accident of their birthplace. In conferring preference and high office the crown, convinced that the atmosphere of relative freedom and affluence in the Indies could breed only a less than perfect Spaniard, consistently favored the home-grown, namely, the *peninsulares*. Despite proven ability, knowledge of the country and its problems, a record of loyal services, and even great wealth, few *criollos* made it to the top. For example, only 4 of the total 127 viceroys were nonpeninsular born, and only 14 *criollos* were among the 602 governors and captains-general. Although there were proportionately a few more Americans among the bishops and archbishops, the ratio was distressingly low.

Below the *criollos* were the mestizos, the offspring of mixed European and Indian lineage, quickly a very numerous class. The early Spanish explorers and conquerors, arriving with that exploiter mentality of get-rich-quick and return home rich, came without their women. American opportunity quickly changed their thinking; they were thoroughly willing to remain exploiters and enjoy their riches in the colony. At any rate, there was much racial intermingling with the Indian women. The resulting situation was of much concern to the early churchmen who sought to regularize these unions for the good both of the souls of those involved and also the offspring. Very soon the crown withdrew its opposition to such unions. The mestizo became an integral part of colonial society.

The male mestizo found himself in the ambiguous position of being less than well received by his father's people but, on the other hand, considering himself better than those of his mother's race. As a result he was left without a firm base from which to operate. His sister fared much better, for her share of white blood gave her an advantage, even an acceptability, in a society short on women.

It was largely left to the mestizo himself whether to choose the road of mobility upward or to resign himself to the second-level position in which birth had located him. The ambitious and energetic could and often did rise. The time even came when the more successful were able to obtain patents to prove themselves *gentes de razón,* that is "white folks." A sizable number of mestizos found opportunity on the frontiers, where a society fighting to survive or building itself paid more heed to what a man could contribute than to blood or other antecedents. Many, however, discouraged and broken by the discrimination encountered, drifted into the ranks of the poor.

The mestizo was regularly more favored than his fellow mixed-breed, the mulatto, offspring of European and African. The mulatto always bore the social taint of his strain of slave blood. They were to be found in all geographic areas of Latin America, but the majority were in the Caribbean islands and Brazil, as African slaves were most numerous in these areas. As freedmen in Brazil they could and did rise to a status of some importance; more rarely was this their lot in the Spanish provinces.

The two pureblood colored groups, Indians and Africans, remained in a state of dependence and on the lower rungs of the social ladder. In the case of the Indians, legally free vassals of the crown, this dependence was of a practical nature. As already noted they were protected, in theory, by royal laws and decrees, which were sometimes enforced and observed. They were most effectively protected by the missionaries who constantly struggled to shield them from the colonials. In some provinces they were able to maintain their own villages in distant places. When forced into the white man's society, they very regularly ended in the *barrios* on the edge of the colonial towns.

The Latin colonials, Spanish particularly, did keep great numbers of Indians alive, and today they account for a not inconsiderable proportion of the population in a number of the nations. Unquestionably, religious conviction entered into this humane policy. With much reminding and no little prodding by churchmen the Spaniards came to accept the Indians as fellow humans, with rights as children of God and brothers of Christ. But such noble motivation was not necessarily the whole story. The Indian was the Spaniards' most available and ready source of labor; hence, it was to their advantage to consider "the only good Indian" to be the *live* Indian.

The black, everywhere, was at the bottom of the social ladder. The *zambo,* offspring of African and Indian, while a reality was also a "forbidden product" by law; the *zambo* was as such lost in the black mass. Here it should be noted that the practice of human slavery was as old and as universal as man himself, that it had never been completely obliterated in medieval Europe, that Spaniards and Portuguese had long seen human slavery practiced by the Moorish invaders of their home peninsula, and, finally, that the Portuguese of the fifteenth century had simply opened by their African contacts a new source of the human commodity.

Fairly early in the Latin American colonial experience, as the Indian labor force declined in the Caribbean islands or as the natives in Brazil proved inept or intractable, African slaves loomed as the answer to the labor shortage. They could be obtained easily and soon proved to be sturdier and better able to withstand the rigors of work in a tropical setting. By the end of the sixteenth century blacks were being introduced in considerable numbers. In both the islands and Brazil they became an important element of the population not only blood-wise but culture-wise as well. For long it was believed and asserted that the Africans were found almost only in the plantation colonies, but more modern research has shown the Africans much more widely diffused. In the late seventeenth and through the eighteenth century blacks were used extensively in the mining provinces of both colonial empires. For example, in Brazil after the discovery of gold in the backcountry most of the work of ore extraction was done by blacks introduced for that work or transplanted in large numbers from the sugar provines along the littoral.

The preponderant majority of Africans imported were males, brought in to do the heavy labor. Some females were sent over but generally were used in domestic service, which often included a measure of "night work." Rounded up in the interior of Africa by native war parties or by native and/or Moslem traders, the unfortunate captives were herded to coastal stations, sold and crowded into ships, and brought to American ports as merchandise for sale. Mortality in the process was high, and for those who survived life expectancy was often only from five to ten years. This generally did not worry the buyers since the supply seemed inexhaustible.

In fairness it should be asserted that within the framework of this brutal institution Latin masters often had some measure of greater compassion than slave owners in later American empires. Many tried to give their slaves at least a veneer of Christianity and allowed at times a glimmer of real humanity to color their treatment and attitudes. But, even so, the African was from first to last a slave, a chattel possession.

As is evident, colonial society in Latin America was dominated by the white or the near-white, if one can so describe the more industrious and prosperous mestizo, or in the terminology of the day by the *gentes de razón*. Not all whites shared the same opulence and affluence. Life in the smaller towns could be dull and existence on the frontier rugged, tough, and dangerous. But there were always greater rewards than could ever have been hoped for back in mother countries. Colonial society was *criollo*-dominated; they were the *ricos,* with the *castas,* the colored elements, playing the role of the poor.

5

How the Colonials Made a Living

Just living, rather than making a living, was the prime goal of primitive man. Using what nature offered, he hunted, fished, or gathered for his sustenance. In time he ingeniously developed things to help him do the job more efficiently. The hunter fashioned his spear and invented the bow and arrow; the fisher, his harpoon hooks, nets, and weirs; the gatherer, bags and basketry. Next, hunters learned to tame some of the animals which they previously secured only by the chance of the chase, while gatherers discovered the secret of the seed and began to grow seeds and plants under controllable conditions. With only a portion of the population, the farmers, needed to ensure the food supply, others could be free to pursue different activities. The day dawned for the specialist, and so did the day of making a living.

The earth continued as man's great resource. Exploiting its subsoil, rich in metals and minerals, coal and petroleum, man became a miner, an extracter. Cultivating its topsoil made him into a farmer. Breeding its animals turned him into a stockman. Other specialists, too, came into being. There was the trader who moved an overabundance or surplus from the point of accumulation to another location where a demand needed supplying. There was the merchant who undertook to distribute this surplus, once arrived. Between them these two specialists laid the basis for commerce. Other men learned to process the grain by grinding it into flour, or to shape the timber into more usable lengths, or to turn the metals into tools; these men were the artisans or manufacturers. Under these five basic heads man's making-a-living activities can be classified—mining, agriculture, stock raising, commerce, and manufacturing.

The Latin American colonials engaged in all of these activities, either personally or what was more usual as directors of the labor of others, namely, the Indians or African slaves. The subsoil in many areas was remarkably rich. The topsoil, quite regularly blessed by a favorable climate, was fertile and productive. It is a matter of some debate as to whether mining or agriculture deserves top rank as the source of colonial prosperity. The vast open lands of the Americas, very frequently covered with lush grasses or other possible fodder made stockbreeding and the related pastoral industries profitable occupations. Commerce and the exchange of things enriched some colonials, but the character of restrictive royal regulation prevented the emergence of a strong and numerous merchant class. The fact that few New World products, other than gold and silver, sugar and tobacco, cacao and drugs, and to some extent hides, were on the export list in any sizable quantity also contributed to making the merchant prince a rare individual. Added to this was the fact that imports were supplied by royally favored Spaniards, thus leaving no room for colonial participation.

● **Mining**

Through the colonial centuries hundreds of millions in gold and silver came from the mines of the Spanish and Portuguese American empires. Total figures are never likely to be found. Official homeland figures ordinarily account only for the king's share of the bullion coming in from the royal *quinto,* with no hint given of the treasure going to private individuals. In the colonies the figures from the mints include only the amounts turned in for registry; there is no way of determining how much ore never got that far. With those qualifications made, here are a few indicative figures: Between 1503 and 1660 officially registered imports into Spain note around 200 tons of fine gold and 18,000 tons of fine silver, while an estimate of output of silver from the mines of Potosí (Upper Bolivia) runs to 800,000,000 pesos.

Gold came chiefly from Mexico, Peru-Bolivia, and Nueva Granada (Colombia), and in the eighteenth century from Brazil's backcountry. Its total, even in value, never exceeded that of the silver mined. In fact, reputed Spanish "gold" was largely silver. Even so, the yield of the mines long made the king of Spain the richest monarch in Europe, and for a time at least the most powerful and most feared. In the later sixteenth and into the seventeenth century the precious-metal output of the Latin American mines worked a price revolution throughout Europe. The mines made many colonial millionaires; they made possible great, if somewhat gaudy, American cities, built stately mansions and dozens of public buildings and churches, sometimes of considerable magnificence even in the lesser towns.

The Spaniards regularly did the prospecting themselves, and in the very early years the actual mining. But very soon this heavy work was turned over to the Indians, serving on *repartimiento* detail. When such use of the natives was forbidden by the crown, the Spaniards resorted to black slave labor. However, in the later seventeenth century the system known as the *cuatequil* was instituted, under which an Indian might voluntarily work in the mines for higher wages. From his accumulated income the Indian was expected both to sustain himself and his family, as well as to save his tribute money. Likely to be improvident, the Indian often had to borrow from his employer for one or other, or both, obligations and go hopelessly into debt. Some students of Indian labor practice claim that this *cuatequil* system, rather than the *repartimiento* or *encomienda*, was the real creator of Indian peonage.

The huge silver enterprise, not surprisingly, gave birth to new ore reduction processes, most notable of which was the so-called *patio* method. A certain Bartolomé de Medina, using findings of German and Flemish experts, perfected the method and introduced it into New Spain shortly after mid-sixteenth century. Most successful there, it spread to the other mining colonies. The silver ore was ground into powder, mixed with mercury, then wetted down and trampled by animals in a large contained area, or patio, until a thick mud-like mass developed. The subsequent furnace smelting oxidized the mercury and left the silver in quite pure form to be shaped into bars. The new and enormous need for mercury greatly expanded Spanish mining prospecting to search for mercury mines. They had good fortune in several areas, but most especially in the rich deposits found at Huancavelica in Peru.

● **Agriculture**

Even though the number of Spaniards and Portuguese working personally as farmers was never large, agriculture was an economic activity equal in importance to mining. As landowners, the conquistadores and their fellows were responsible for the development. There was land aplenty, and both crowns were generous with grants, these ranging from smaller plots given to all whites who requested them to hundreds and thousands of acres offered to colonists whom kings wished especially to favor. From the beginning these lands were worked by native labor and later by a sizable proportion of African slave labor. Actually only on the frontier did the colonist do much of his own work, except for the poorer whites in the more settled areas. When much labor was available the greater landlords very much resembled the medieval lords of Europe, masters of the land and a whole family of dependents. This situation prevailed quite universally in the sugar plantations of Brazil and in the Spanish provinces where cultivation of the land was the chief source of wealth, as, for example, in Chile.

Almost everywhere in Latin America the natives long before the conquest grew maize or Indian corn as the chief bread grain—in the tropical forests of the Amazon country, climatically unfavorable to maize production, the Indians had manioc or the cassava root as their bread substance. The Europeans encouraged continuation of the native practice and, thanks to the better tools which they brought, production was greatly increased. Through most of the colonial period maize constituted the principal bread grain for natives and whites alike. Though produced in quantity, maize was rarely exported.

The colonists learned to eat and enjoy several of the other products of Indian agriculture, such as beans, various members of the gourd family, peppers, and the white potato. This last, domesticated along the Andean cordillera, in time became, perhaps, the most important American agricultural contribution to the European diet. There were other American agricultural contributions in various categories: yams, tomatoes, cacao, peanuts; coca (cocaine) and cinchona (quinine) in the drug class; also chicle and rubber. It has been remarked facetiously that it must have been dull at sporting contests in Europe before the discovery of America, with no peanuts or popcorn, cigars or cigarettes, chewing gum and chocolate candy bars.

Many Old World products were introduced and often cultivated extensively in Latin America. Notable were grains and cereals such as wheat, oats, barley, millet; sugar cane, rice, bananas, and later coffee were brought over, all of which did well in the New

World. The Europeans also brought many fruits, especially those of the citrus family, vegetables, and nuts. Wheat, most important at least from the European point of view, could not be grown everywhere, nor could rice. Outdistancing all imports in economic value was sugar cane. Sugar quickly became the most important American agricultural export commodity.

There were several European imports which had interesting histories in the colonies, the vine and olive and mulberry trees. Wine grapes of good quality were cultivated particularly in Chile and parts of Mexico. Fearing developing competition, at least on the American market, Spanish vintners pushed the crown to forbid or, at very least, seriously to restrict colonial wine-making. The olive tree found hospitable soil and growing conditions in Peru. Home interests likewise forced a royal ban, but it was not as rigidly enforced as that against the vine. Quite early Dominican friars introduced the mulberry tree into their missions in southern Mexico. The silk industry of Oaxaca had a thriving period, but it was cut short by competition from silk from the Orient, brought back by the Manila galleon.

The introduction of Old World tools and techniques, when coupled with varied lands and climates overseas, did much to make colonial agriculture a profitable economic enterprise. The immediate returns may not have been as fabulous as those of mining, but in the long run agriculture made many colonials economically comfortable, and also allowed the Indians to share in this good fortune.

The landowning "aristocracy" which developed was predominantly *criollo* and sometimes mestizo in make-up. Agriculture created a strong class in overseas society. Its members did not have political power or even top-rank social position, but they did have the very real potential power of wealth. With the passing years these men became the backbone of the dissatisfaction which grew up against an unyielding royal power.

● **Stock Raising**

Another economic activity which contributed to colonial making-a-living was the pastoral industry. Interestingly, it often was the road to riches for the less fortunate *criollos* and ambitious mestizos, who had not been able to make it into the great land-owner class.

The Spaniards, even as they migrated to the Americas, were accomplished stockmen. Centuries before their coming to the New World, Moorish invaders had introduced this tradition into their home peninsula. Beginning with the second voyage of Columbus the transfer of Old World domesticated animals began. Hogs and cattle prospered in the islands, although the horse did less well there. All three, plus sheep and goats, the donkey and the mule, went to the mainland with the conquistadores. Not only did the familiar animals give the Spaniards a certain sense of security in their strange new lands, they also worked a definite revolution in the way of life of the Indians who had existed through the preceding centuries without large domesticated food or draft animals. Cattle and hogs, and some of the others, furnished a new element, and a stable one, in the food range of the Americans, eliminating the chance of the chase and, in areas, the resort to cannibalism in the effort to ensure the meat supply in their diet. Further, the mountable animals furnished new means of locomotion. Draft animals, especially when combined with the wheeled vehicles which the Spaniards introduced, gave new transportation potential everywhere but particularly in areas where the waterways, primitive man's nature-made "highways," failed to solve the need of getting from one place to another. This was often the case in Latin America with its great open spaces and its towering mountains. Movement by foot and freighting by human carrier no longer remained the only way of travel and transportation. Stock raising could and did become a big business enterprise serving multiple needs and goods.

The horse was the prize animal, in the towns, in the countryside, and on the frontier. Initially, however, it was a "status" mount, reserved for the white man, forbidden to the Indian. Although this prohibition long remained on the books, in time enforcement relaxed and the Indian, especially on the frontier, did obtain the horse. Spaniards loved and were proud of their horses, bred them carefully, and often spent lavishly for saddles and accoutrements.

Cattle were raised primarily for food, and the same was true of the lesser stock. Mules and oxen were the prime draft animals. The burro became an all-purpose animal for the Indians; they were affordable and not infrequently attained what was almost pet status in the family. In some areas sheep were bred, primarily for their wool.

Cattle-raising brought into being a special breed of man, the cowboy. In northern New Spain he was the *vaquero,* in the Orinoco basin the *llanero,* in the river-plains provinces of the south the *gaucho.* Very often these were mestizos. The missionaries on various frontiers had small herds and taught their Indians to know, tend, and breed the animals, giving a new dimension to their lives.

In the Andes the Indians were encouraged to continue to breed their own domesticated animals of preconquest days. However, the llama, the vicuña, and the alpaca were raised for their wool, rather than for hard work.

● **Commerce**

From many of the things already noted above, it should be rather evident that the trader in colonial Latin America worked under a number of handicaps imposed by royal restrictions and regulations. To these can be added those of a physical nature imposed by geography.

The importing trader was very much at the mercy of the monopolists of Seville who were his suppliers. Their shipments not infrequently might not reach the Indies, in which case the American trader was left without goods, for a longer or shorter time. When the goods did arrive, he had to pick them up at the designated port, whether it was convenient to him or not. Then he faced the problem of transporting his goods inland. In this process he either had to have a large capital investment in wagons, carts, and pack animals, or be dependent on yet another middle man who furnished these. In one way or another the prices he had to charge were regularly very high, and this could be a factor in controlling the demand which he was endeavoring to serve. For example goods destined for Buenos Aires, in days before that South American port was opened, had to originate in Spain. There was the long sea voyage to Portobelo, the transfer across the Isthmus, another sea voyage to Callao, then the long overland haul, up the Andes to the *altiplano,* thence down into the plains country. The haul for Peru or Nueva Granada or Mexico was not as long, but many hands were involved and also many risks.

The domestic trader had to face the problems of local geography only, but these were regularly tremendous, poor roads, dangers to goods in transit, and the vagaries of carriers. Little wonder that he expected to be recompensed for the risks involved.

The local merchant or shopkeeper always had the problem of supply, from overseas, from intraprovince sources, and even from local or nearby artisans.

When all the factors are considered, it is little wonder that trade and commerce were not among the more attractive ways of making a living.

● Manufacturing

This was not a highly developed colonial activity, save in the area of simple production to serve the most basic of needs—furniture, tools and simple household requirements, clothing and rough textiles, and other things in this category. Neither Spaniards nor Portuguese at home had had much of a manufacturing tradition to pass on to colonists overseas. In the case of Spain, during their drive for religious unity, kings had expelled Moors and Jews who through the centuries had carried on this sort of work.

Interestingly, some of the best manufacturing in the Indies was done by the Indians. The colonials recognized them as accomplished weavers, excellent potters, ingenious silver- and goldsmiths, and in instances, as in the case of the tilemakers of Puebla (Mexico), producers of things both useful and beautiful. Officials encouraged the natives to continue their arts and crafts. Unfortunately, however, Spanish greed in time entered the picture and Indian craftsmen were often gathered in *obrages* under sweatshop conditions to carry on large-scale production, this as a work obligation under the *repartimiento*.

The absence of manufacturing development during the colonial period, even though raw materials were available in abundance, was one of the serious deficiencies in the economic life of the Indies. The later Latin American nations which grew out of the colonies would long be hampered thereby in the modern world in which they had to compete. Too long they continued as raw-materials producers in the rapidly developing industrialized economy. Imperial Spain and Portugal had been content to let them remain such.

Mercantilism was not designed to prepare colonies ultimately to become independent nations. Colonial economies should be judged in that framework. Spain and Portugal were no different in applying mercantilist principles than their rivals in the older colonial world. The future phenomenal success of England's former colonies in North America as independent nations was not exactly the intent of her colonial policies.

6

The Church in the Indies

Perhaps no one of the institutions transplanted to the colonial world by Spain and Portugal left so deep an imprint on the future Latin Americas as the Catholic Church. Nothing was more natural to the Iberian peoples of the sixteenth century than to wish to share their Christian faith with their fellow subjects overseas. The obligation to do so had been emphasized by Pope Alexander VI as one of the conditions for his confirmation of the claims made by Columbus in the name of the Crown of Castile. Most Spaniards took that obligation seriously and, went to their New World with a certain crusading zeal. At times this noble resolve seemed and was deeply submerged by other less admirable attitudes, but it was always present underneath. One facet of the conquistador character was that of the crusading apostle.

The Spaniards were rather uniquely fitted for this role of Christian apostles. Through the medieval centuries the Spaniards had battled the Moorish invaders of their peninsula. In those days Spanish nationalism and Christianity became very nearly synonymous terms. Ferdinand and Isabella had just concluded the "last crusade," when the *capitulación* (contract) with Columbus was signed under the walls of the last Moorish stronghold, Granada. The Spaniards were, so to speak, temporarily "unemployed" and available for a new Christian venture.

The church in Spain, which had constantly been a partner in the long crusade, was especially strong and in favor. Further, it was strengthened by the recent reforms engineered by the monarch's minister and powerful adviser, Cardinal Jiménez de Cisneros, and this, very significantly, in a day when Christian faith elsewhere in Europe was cooling and showing serious need of rejuvenation. Spain, the Spaniards, and the Spanish church were uniquely ready for the new challenge.

● The Patronato Real

This is the term by which the church-state relationship is designated. The flow of churchmen began with the second voyage of Columbus, in 1493. The first came primarily to serve the spiritual needs of the colonists, but before long the crown was sending Franciscans and Dominicans to undertake the conversion of the natives. Quickly the monarchs came to recognize the enormity of the task they had accepted, and also its expense. When they appealed to the pope for financial assistance, Alexander VI sanctioned a special tax on church funds. Next, he gave the monarchs the right to collect the tithes, the normal church tax on all the faithful, and to disburse those moneys for the support of the colonial church and the work of evangelization of the natives. Then, in 1502, by his bull *Universalis ecclesiae regiminis* Pope Julius II granted the monarch of Spain the full right of patronage over the colonial church, the *Patronato Real*.

The *patronato* for the New World was patterned on the extensive rights and privileges granted to Ferdinand and Isabella by Innocent VIII in 1485, in the so-called Bull of Granada, as they readied the "last crusade" against the Moors in the peninsula. Besides the permission to collect and use the tithes, the Spanish monarch was given the right to nominate candidates for major ecclesiastical offices, such as bishops, to supervise the clergy, to give permission for the construction of churches, to erect and delimit dioceses, and to control all missionary efforts. When later Spanish monarchs added to these extensive powers certain arrogated "rights," such as that of screening all papal laws, decrees, and letters pertinent to church affairs overseas, the king became something of a lay pope for the Indies, a sort of senior partner in the crown-church relationship. To the credit of the Spanish kings it should be noted that no one of them, even though these powers were jealously guarded and regularly exercised, overstepped the bounds of propriety in order to meddle in matters of dogma and doctrine.

There were advantages as well as disadvantages in this arrangement from the church's point of view. The church was relieved of the necessity of raising the basic funds with which to operate, for these were furnished from the royal treasury. Further, royal absolutism relieved the church from having to compete with other Christian sects, since Roman Catholicism was the only accepted state religion and all others were outlawed. However, there were times when royal interference rendered life uncomfortable, especially when it tended to cut down what could have been very salutary supervisory control by Rome. Some of the abuses in the colonial church can be traced to this very nearly all-pervading lay or secular control; others, to be sure, had abundant roots in fallen human nature. But, good or bad, the *patronato* system endured, a regime of close union of church and state.

● **The "Urban Church"**

In the Latin American story the missionary aspect of the work of the church, dramatic, exciting, broadly publicized, has tended to eclipse the functioning of what might be termed the "urban church." In many ways it was this church rather than the missionary or "frontier church" which was most influential in shaping life and manners. Often overlooked is the strong and constant impact of the pastoral and sacramental aspects of the clergy's work with the Spaniards. The social-service ministries, for the poor, the sick and the infirm, the widows and orphans, served as a constant reminder of the obligation of Christian charity. The very presence of men and women whose lives were dedicated to the pursuit of the higher values had a salutary effect on colonial life.

The colonials, rich and poor, devoted and scoundrels, did have a deep and often very active faith which manifested itself in varied ways. The multiplicity of churches, monasteries, and *conventos*, hospitals and hospices, many of them splendid and richly decorated, stand as enduring testimonials to that faith. Like the medieval cathedrals many hands helped to build these structures, and all residents had a pride and a certain proprietary interest in them. The elaborate churches and religious buildings in most instances are simply more grandiose and even gaudy and overdecorated copies of baroque and rococo models of the homeland.

● **The Wealth of the Church**

Not all the wealth was tied up in the great buildings, or in the rich altar vessels, or in the art adorning the churches and monasteries. Much of the church wealth consisted of vast landholdings. Very early the church was the beneficiary of royal generosity. Then as time ran, grants of land, sometimes extensive, were made by pious individuals and at others by the less pious who thought thus to make amends for transgressions and who sought the prayers of the church after their deaths. The accumulation was considerable, so much so that by the end of the colonial period the church in many areas was the greatest and richest landowner. This was significant in a society in which land was the most universal form of wealth.

Much more of the varied wealth of the church than is regularly recognized went to support its many ministries, especially those of a social-service character. It is true that not a few of the ecclesiastics who administered this wealth acted as though they were the real owners and lived lives accordingly.

● The Church and Education

Another involvement of the colonial church in Latin American life was in the field of education. Prior to the nineteenth century, education was universally regarded throughout the Western world as a duty and responsibility of the church. The colonial church, heir to the tradition of the monastic and cathedral schools of the Feudal Age and of the universities of the High Middle Ages, undertook this work in the Indies as a matter of course.

Just past mid-sixteenth century royal charters were requested and issued for the first two American universities. The Universidad de México opened almost immediately; that of San Marcos in Lima began formally two decades later. By the end of the colonial period Spanish America could boast of ten major and fifteen "minor" universities.

No system of universal primary education was developed. There were some schools for the sons of the whites and a few for the sons of Indian chiefs (*caciques*) who seemed to have the potential to grow into leaders of their people. It should be remembered in this connection that universal primary education, for either boys or girls, was not common in the Western world until the French Revolution and after; hence, the Spanish Indies simply reflected European practice in this regard.

In the mission schools, while there was no great emphasis on the "three R's," the Indian youngsters were given considerable vocational or technical training. The range might be from simple carpentry to stock raising. Probably most important was the acquaintance given to the use and value of the white man's tools.

Until the arrival of the Jesuits, in Peru in the 1560s and in Mexico in the 1570s, there was a gap between the existing primary education and that of the universities. The Jesuit *colegios* filled that vacuum—the *colegio* would be the equivalent of the modern high school and junior college.

As in Europe of the day, the teachers and professors were regularly clerics, priests or religious of the orders. The pattern for the universities was also European. In the Indies the model was the Universidad de Salamanca, a Spanish offshoot of the older and more famous University of Paris. The major universities had the traditional faculties, or schools, of arts, philosophy-theology, medicine, civil law and canon (church) law. As an indication of colonial interest and patronage, the following figures for degrees granted by the University of Mexico can be enlightening: theology, 937; canon law, 491; civil law, 104; medicine, 180; arts, 134. At the University of Mexico in the earlier period there was a chair of Indian languages. In the eighteenth century the university curriculum was broadened a bit, to include the developing interest in science, but to the end the universities continued to be conservatively traditional. Whatever study there may have been of the new trends in science, in philosophy, in politico-economic thought, was carried on in the *academias*, beyond the university cloisters.

The Portuguese of Brazil were less education-minded than their Spanish neighbors. Brazil had no colonial university. Parents desiring advanced education for their sons sent them to the University of Coimbra in the mother country or elsewhere in Europe. Brazil did have a few Jesuit *colegios* in the major cities.

● **The Inquisition**

The Holy Office of the Inquisition was introduced into the Indies in the latter part of the sixteenth century, but delegates of the office had been operating much earlier. This institution at home, since its foundation in the 1480s, had been a powerful agency of both crown and church for maintaining orthodoxy of belief and practice. It really was part of the royal drive for absolutist control over all aspects of Spanish life and, as such, was a political as well as a religious instrument of the crown. Early it was designed to bring into line Moors and Jews and lapsed converts from these faiths; later its power was turned against dissenters from the Catholic position in faith and morals, in a word non-Catholics.

In the colonies, as at home, the Inquisition was the watchdog of Catholic belief, and also of public and especially clerical morality. The colonial Inquisition was never given jurisdiction over the Indians or over the blacks; only the whites and near-whites were the objects of its attention. It had to deal with relatively few non-Catholic heretics in the Indies, given the royal prohibition against immigration of all but orthodox Catholics. For example, during the 293 years of its informal and then formal existence in New Spain (Mexico), only 43 so-called *relajados* were turned over to the secular arm for summary punishment and the figure was similar in South America.

The inquisitors and principal assistants were churchmen. They heard the cases of whites reported for suspicious and/or Protestant ideas and practices or for heinous and scandalous moral conduct. The inquisitors had the power to imprison the guilty or even to exile them from the colony, to exact fines, and to impose public penitential punishments. The Holy Office was feared and its existence did serve as a check not only on the public expression of doctrinal dissent, but also on illegal moral practice, among both the clergy and the laity of whatever rank or status.

In the eighteenth century, when the crown felt that the ideas of the Enlightenment coming in from Europe might seriously threaten its position overseas, the Inquisition, along with its other competences, was turned into an agency for the censorship of books entering the Indies. Toward the end of that century, as part of the Bourbon reforms, the Inquisition was abolished.

In judging the Spanish Inquisition it seems fair to remember that it was frequently used as a political arm of the absolutist crown to strike down the royal enemies within the realm. Further, it operated in an age of universal intolerance, not only of religious dissent but also of political disagreement, at a time when religion and nationalism were often linked and when freedom of thought was not then part of the culture in the Western world.

● **The Missionary or "Frontier Church"**

Most of what has been noted to this point concerning the work of the church touched the lives of the white and near-white classes. The church left its imprint on attitudes, manners, and morals, and as a consequence was a powerful force in shaping Latin American character and outlook. These classes, no matter how important in fact, formed only a relatively small segment of the population. Besides there were hundreds of thousands of Indians whose lives the church sought to influence with the Christian gospel and way of life. And she had some success in leaving a stamp on them as well.

As frontiers pushed out into the hinterlands, a new challenge to Spanish evangelizing zeal developed. The frontiersmen encountered Indians much less tractable, less civilized, and not ready to be dominated or Christianized. Practices which had worked with the peoples of the empires were thoroughly ineffective. These Indians were nonsedentary. They had not been conditioned to provide personal labor services nor to pay tribute to overlords. More than that, they were inclined to disrupt the wealth-gathering activities of the conquerors.

By late sixteenth century the mission had become a Spanish frontier institution for pacification, Christianization, Hispanicization, and expansion. It worked well on many frontiers in both continents. It turned the nomad and seminomad into a sedentary farmer and acquainted him with many of the material things which the Spaniard had to give, most importantly domesticated animals, new food seeds and grains, more efficient tools, improved crafts and techniques. The missionary did not forget that he was first and foremost an apostle of the Christian gospel, but he could be a teacher of other less lofty things as well. The mission was a many-sided agency.

The "frontier church" touched the lives of thousands, sometimes deeply and at others only superficially, but it left a mark on Indian populations throughout Latin America which has endured.

7

The Bourbon Century

The eighteenth century opened with Spain under new management. The House of the Spanish Hapsburgs died out in 1700, with the passing of Charles II. By much maneuvering the powerful Louis XIV of France managed to seat his grandson, Philippe d'Anjou, on the Spanish throne and thus begin the line of Spanish Bourbons. A bitter European war was fought before the powers of Europe accepted this arrangement, the War of the Spanish Succession, 1702-13.

The year of the Treaty of Utrecht, 1713, which brought an end to that war, is one of those so-called watershed dates in the history of the Western world. It definitely saw an end to the threat of French hegemony in Europe, which had been present during much of the long reign of Louis XIV. That year just as certainly marked an early milepost in the rise of England, both in Europe and overseas. Even though Spain sustained certain setbacks by terms of the treaty, that power was left with a glimmer of hope that better days were ahead, such as Spain had not known since her "Golden Age" in the sixteenth century, which ended with the passing of Philip II.

The first Spanish Bourbons set to work energetically but centered most of their attention and effort on regaining prestige in Europe. Not until after mid-century, during the 1759-88 reign of Charles III, did royal effort turn toward the Indies. Vital, however, as the Bourbon reforms would be for the empire, they are only one aspect of the eighteenth century events affecting Latin America.

● **International Rivalries**

Perhaps the most far-reaching of these developments was the increasing involvement of Spain in the international rivalries at work in the colonial world. Four European powers had American empires, Spain and Portugal, France and England, and Holland had a few Caribbean islands and a small chunk of northeastern South America, Dutch Guiana or Surinam. Through the seventeenth-century decades the Spaniards had to content themselves with making their American possessions more and more Spanish and in building protection by the expansion of frontiers.

The English were edging southward from Carolina bases toward Spanish Florida and in the next century actually occupied Georgia. The French, as the seventeenth century closed, appeared on the Gulf of Mexico Coast, first at Biloxi and a few years later moved eastward to the more strategic Mobile. The French at Mobile were not worrisome until in 1714 Louis Juchereau de Saint-Denis and several companions suddenly appeared at Misión San Juan Bautista on the Rio Grande—they had come overland from the recently founded French post of Natchitoches on the Red River. At that point Spain revised her frontier thinking and in 1716 moved eastward to turn Texas into a defensive buffer province.

In the southern continent the Portuguese moving beyond the Tordesillas Line complicated life for the Spaniards. In 1724 the Spaniards crossed the Río de la Plata estuary and founded Montevideo. From this base they sought to counter the Portuguese activities in the Banda Oriental, which for several decades past had centered around their Colônia del Sacramento, set farther up the estuary. Not only were the Portuguese territorial trespassers, they were also using Colônia as a depot for extensive smuggling activities.

Beginning in 1769 the Spaniards in the northern continent made a defensive move against the Russians, threatening to extend southward from Alaska. This was the occupation of Alta California. New interest in the Pacific Coast Spain also saw as a means of forestalling possible English westward expansion from Canada, which Britain had obtained from France by the Peace of Paris of 1763. All this West Coast activity was closely tied to Spanish desire to protect the homebound route of her important and profitable trade with the Orient via the Pacific.

Further, during the Bourbon Century Spain was on a number of occasions embroiled in the long series of struggles sometimes designated as the "Second Hundred Years War." The perennial antagonists were France and Britain, but because almost all of these wars in Europe had an American counterpart Spain became involved as one of the ranking colonial powers. In these conflicts Spain's fortunes varied.

By the Treaty of Utrecht which closed the War of the Spanish Succession (Queen Anne's War in the colonies), Spain as a result of being on the losing side saw her monopoly of trade to her own colonies weakened. She had to yield to England the *asiento* or slave-trade contract for a period of years, and the English were granted the right to send an annual ship, the *navío de permiso*, loaded with merchandise to the fairs at Vera Cruz and Portobelo. Having gained a toehold, the English sought to expand trade advantages in American waters and engaged in much smuggling. When Spain forcibly objected in the later 1730s, she and England had their War of Jenkins' Ear—this belligerency fused into King George's War (War of the Austrian Succession in Europe). Next, as a partner of France by terms of the so-called Family Compact, Spain was pulled into the last phases of the French and Indian War, and lost Cuba to the British. In the Peace of Paris (1763) Spain had to redeem Cuba by ceding Florida to England. In late 1762, wishing as much to preserve the territory from falling into English hands as to recompense Spain for losses sustained, France practically forced on her the Trans-Mississippi half of Louisiana. During the War of the American Revolution Spain, formally as an ally of France and not of the revolting English colonies, helped to make life miserable for the English. This time being on the winning side, in the Peace of Paris of 1783 she regained the Floridas and control of the complete Gulf of Mexico coastline. But very soon she was squabbling with the Americans over the international boundary in the southern Trans-Allegheny, and control of the Mississippi. The resolution of this latter question in the Treaty of San Lorenzo (1795) was something of a diplomatic humiliation. Spain's troubles in North America were compounded when in 1800 Napoleon demanded the retrocession of Louisiana to France and then in 1803 double-crossed the Spaniards by selling the Trans-Mississippi to the young United States, making the pushy Americans actual neighbors to Texas and potential neighbors to New Mexico.

● **Bourbon Reforms**

Another very significant aspect of the Bourbon Century was the institution of a number of reforms in colonial administration and control. These came largely in the second half of the eighteenth century, after the accession of Charles III, and were reflections of the liberalizing tendencies of the Age of the Benevolent/Enlightened Despots.

The two original administrative divisions of the Spanish Empire, the viceroyalty of New Spain for North America and the viceroyalty of Peru for the whole of South America, had become unwieldy and almost impossible to manage efficiently.

In the southern continent, where change was needed more desperately, the single viceroyalty was split into three, that of Peru, that of Nueva Granada (1740), and, finally, that of Buenos Aires (1776). Chile and Venezuela were raised to the rank of captaincies-general which reported directly to the Council of the Indies and the crown. There was also a semi-independent frontier jurisdiction, known as the Comandancia de Las Maynas, set up on the eastern slope of the cordillera.

In North America, as of 1776, the northern provinces of New Spain were withdrawn from the direct control of the viceroy at Mexico City and formed into an administrative unit known as the Commandancy-General of the Interior Provinces. The *comandante* was to live on the frontier, so as to be in closer touch with the problems he was expected to solve. He was to be primarily concerned with the defense of his vast area against the Indians who were disrupting the life of the frontier, the troublesome Apaches and the even fiercer Comanches who were rampaging and threatening the important "silver provinces" closer in. Interestingly, when Spanish Louisiana was acquired, it was not joined to the Interior Provinces but assigned to the jurisdiction of Havana, where Cuba was raised to the rank of an independent captaincy-general. This was a realistic decision since Louisiana and the middle-valley settlements were Gulf of Mexico oriented, and had little, if anything, to do with Mexico.

More important, even, in the area of colonial administration was the introduction of the *intendencia*—first established in Havana (1764), then extended to Buenos Aires in 1782, to Peru in 1784, to New Spain and Chile in 1786, and throughout the rest of the empire in 1790. New Spain, for example, was divided into

VICEROYALTY OF NEW SPAIN

Provincias Internas

Louisiana

Florida

ATLANTIC

Ciudad Mexico   Vera Cruz

Habana

Captaincy General of Cuba

OCEAN

Guatemala

Captaincy General of Guatemala

VICEROYALTY OF NEW GRANADA

Caracas

Captaincy General of Caracas

Audiencia of Santa Fe de Bogota

Bogota

GUIANA

Quito

Presidency of Quito

Las Maynas

Callao

Lima

VICEROYALTY OF PERU

Cuzco

Presidency of Charcas

BRAZIL

Pernambuco

Salvador

PACIFIC

Asuncion

Rio de Janeiro

OCEAN

Tucuman

Santiago

Mendoza

Captaincy General & Presidency of Chile

LA PLATA

Audiencia of Buenos Aires

Buenos Aires

VICEROYALTY OF

LATIN AMERICA IN THE LATE EIGHTEENTH CENTURY

twelve intendencies, each in charge of an *intendente*, who in turn was assisted by a number of *subdelegados*. The system was designed to regularize into a set pattern the local and provincial administration and to centralize control and responsibility. Thus the intendents were to replace the multiplicity and diversity of earlier municipal and provincial officials.

The intendent was a busy man and, presumably, versatile as well. He had many functions but the most important were of an economic and financial nature, although he also was vested with some judicial authority, as well as military powers. Among his specific duties were such things as responsibility for promoting agriculture, industry, commerce, stock raising, and even irrigation. He was expected to improve the administration of municipal finances, to see to the cleaning and paving of streets, and to ensure the town water supply. Besides, he was the overseer for the proper operation of granaries and markets, inns, the mints, and bridges. The end of the Spanish regime came before the *intendencia* really had a chance to prove itself, but the early results of this system of centralization did give good promise.

Another accomplishment of Bourbon reform was if not the complete abolition, at very least the alleviation of the smothering control over trade and commerce. The *flota* system of strictly regulated sailings and returnings was discontinued; individual ships were allowed to sail at their convenience; more ports on both sides of the Atlantic were opened; and all Spaniards, along with even some foreigners, were allowed to participate in colonial trade.

● The Enlightenment

The Bourbon reforms were well-intentioned, but time was to prove them too little and too late. Revolutionary ideas were moving faster and pointing farther than even the more liberal of the enlightened despots such as Charles III of Spain were willing to go. These men would make concessions but they wanted to maintain control over how they should be implemented, in a word they were not minded to surrender all power to a group and certainly not to the people's representatives.

As the eighteenth century advanced, the institutional props of the old regime were bit by bit being reasoned away—absolute monarchy, mercantilist economy, rigidly stratified societal patterns, Christianity itself, and what was most destructive of all, the belief that all these were sacrosanct and ordained by God, which had so long prevailed in the West. The scientists, at work since the days of Galileo and Copernicus, were winning new recruits in their drive to test one after another of the traditional "truths"—it was upsetting enough to be told that the universe was actually sun- not earth-centered, but this was only a beginning of long-held convictions to be scrapped. Philosophers sought to maintain the revolutionary pace, and the social scientists joined the pack.

Reason, not authority as through the centuries, was asserted to be the only measuring rod of truth. The natural which could be reached by reason and studied by observation was more compelling and convincing than the supernatural which one had to accept unseen and was probable simply on the word of faith. Existing institutions were being tested by the rule of reason and deemed valid and worthy of human acceptance only after they measured up to the standards of natural law.

A band of highly articulate critics and publicists, the so-called *philosophes*, were commanding wide attention and winning enthusiastic acceptance for their scathing rejection of the society of the old regime. All that was old and traditional was subjected to scrutiny and systematically challenged in the name of science and reason, the new gospel of the day.

As the century ran, the Western world was in a state of ferment. The disgruntled and the dissatisfied, the frustrated and the victims of discrimination, the repressed and the oppressed, all found hope, salvation, even utopia in the new ideas which they were assured were the road to "Progress," which should be the great goal of humankind.

Enlightened though the Spaniards at home may have thought themselves, they were not much in favor of opening their Indies to these new ideas which might well bring an end to the empire which supported them. Yet, despite often vigorous crown effort and the new job given to the Inquisition as censor and policeman, these new ideas did filter into the overseas colonies. John Locke and the English philosophers, as well as their French scholar counterparts, Voltaire and Montesquieu, Diderot and his *Grande Encyclopédie*, and a bit later Jean Jacques Rousseau, came to be known in the Indies. The books of these influential thinkers were smuggled in, sometimes very ingeniously, such as the full set of the *Encyclopédie* which was hidden in the hollow inside of a pious statue. These works were read surreptitiously and discussed even more secretly. At times an occasional daring colonial writer expressed some of these new ideas in his writing, but more regularly they were harbored quietly and allowed to ferment into hopes.

● Signs of Restlessness

Even without the help of the new ideas Latin American colonials were already fretting under the heavy burdens of high taxation, all-pervading regulation, and galling restriction. Periodically from mid-eighteenth century onward dissatisfaction resulted in a show of revolt. The Venezuelans goaded by the heavy exactions of the royally chartered Caracas Company demonstrated belligerently. Somewhat later their neighbors the Granadinos let Viceroy Amar y Borbón know that they did not appreciate the tax boost imposed to finance Spain's involvement in the War of the American Revolution. Royal officials in Chile had to deal with the conspiracy of the "Three Antonios," who had a plan for a real break for independence. José de Antequera and his *comuneros* gave Paraguay a preview of what Latin America would know only too often when a strong man and a few fanatic followers would take over as *caudillos*. Even the despairing Peruvian Indians got into the act, when they made a bid for power under the Inca claimant Tupac Amarú III. Brazil had its young Joaquim José da Silva Xavier, best known as Tiradentes, who plotted revolution and paid with his life for his effort. No one of these stirrings of dissent came to full growth, but each in its own way was symptomatic of the hidden unrest.

● The Revolutionary Frame of Mind

Just as the new ideas stirred a class in Europe, so, too, in Latin America. The *criollos* and the successful mestizos with them, applying to themselves the new ideas, saw no reason why they were not the equals of the highly favored *peninsulares*, why they were ranged in their society as second-class citizens. They found nothing natural, philosophically speaking, about making the geographic accident of birthplace the norm why they should be constantly regulated or why their large contributions to colonial society should not be recognized, honored, and rewarded with highly responsible appointments—the minimal number of *criollos* on the roster of viceroys, captains-general, governors, bishops irked them greatly. The doctrine of natural rights, equality, liberty, and all such struck responsive chords and began to attune them for the rhythm of change.

Then, in quick succession, came two inspiring examples of what the application of these ideas could effect. In the middle 1770s word filtered into Latin America that thirteen of England's American colonies, declaring that all men are created equal, that certain natural rights are self-evident, that the prime function of government was to serve and not to oppress, had challenged the mother country and were making an armed bid for freedom and self-determination. Later the Latins learned that Britain recognized these former colonies as a sovereign nation, the United States of America.

Before the century closed, Frenchmen had revolted in the name of liberty, equality, fraternity. They had overturned the structures of the old regime, beheaded their king, and put themselves under the rule of a government of their own choosing. As a statement of their convictions and goals, the Frenchmen had drawn up a *credo* which they called "The Declaration of the Rights of Man and the Citizen." Copies of this document, as were earlier copies of "The Declaration of Independence," were smuggled into Latin America and circulated among the restless *criollos* in various of the provinces. The French spoke more eloquently to the Latin mind than had the few terse sentences of the Anglo-American statement, but both carried a thrilling message. Besides, the French set the example of overturning a regime and society so very similar to those which the Latin Americans knew and under which they suffered. The Anglo-Americans and the French showed that the new ideas could be implemented.

8

Independence for the Latin Americas

Curiously, the circumstances which sparked the revolutionary explosion in Latin America were wholly European. The causes, to be sure, were American, and with or without European help unrest would probably not have been too long delayed. The mounting temper of the colonials most certainly would have seen to that.

● The European Circumstances

Napoleon, consistently victorious against continental enemies, recognized that he must defeat England to realize his dream of ruling the world. Yet the English Channel put Britain out of reach of his remarkable armies. Without the sea power which he had lost in the Battle of Trafalgar, he was powerless to strike at this archenemy directly. Economic warfare was his only hope. Accordingly, in 1806 he started to build his Continental System, designed to cut England off from her necessary continental markets. Success of this type of warfare was contingent on his ability to maintain the boycott of English goods absolutely airtight.

However, three "leaks" soon showed on the continent. The one in Holland he closed off easily, by summarily removing his brother Louis from the position of king of Holland. The leak through the papal states he plugged after bringing uncooperative Pope Pius VII to Fountainebleau as his prisoner. But there still remained the leak through Portugal, which out of long friendship with England kept her ports open to British goods.

Geography created a major problem for Napoleon as he sought to deal with Portugal. Without a fleet to make a direct attack possible, he had to move overland through Spain. The Spanish crown refused permission. Then the king, Charles IV, had a very serious altercation with his son, soon to be Ferdinand VII. Napoleon took advantage of the situation and offered to act as peacemaker, inviting the two to meet with him at Bayonne. Once there, he held the Spaniards as virtual prisoners. Next, he ordered his armies to move across Spain to strike at Portugal, and installed his brother Joseph as king of Spain. The Spanish people balked, and quickly the opposition stiffened into fierce nationalist resistance behind an interim government known as the Junta Central.

The next years were hectic. The Portuguese resisted determinedly, and Britain spirited the royal family off to Brazil, before Napoleon could take the prince regent and turn him into a compliant puppet. Next door, the Spaniards defied *"el rey intruso,"* King Joseph Bonaparte, and his supporting French forces. Nationalism, that force spawned by the French Revolution in the days of the First Republic and the Directory, boomeranged against the French. Ultimately, Napoleon sustained his first major setback in the peninsula, giving heart to his enemies in Europe by showing that he was not invincible—armed assistance from England greatly helped, but Spanish native resistance was the main cause of the defeat, even though for a time in 1810 it seemed to be broken.

● **The Early American Reaction**

News of what was happening in Spain reached the Indies quickly. Then came emissaries from King Joseph asking for allegiance. The reported maneuver of the Spaniards at home in setting up a temporary government to rule in the name of the detained Ferdinand VII gave the colonials ideas. In some of the provinces the governing *junta*, even though some of the leaders saw it as a possible first step toward independence, was proclaimed to be a purely temporary government functioning in the name of Ferdinand VII. In others, notably Ecuador, Bolivia, and Chile, the leaders talked loudly of independence, and as a result brought on themselves the reprisals of royal officers and garrisons.

Next came *"el año de diez,"* that is 1810. In Spain the resistance movement met temporary setbacks but at the moment it was not clear that it had not been broken. When word reached the Indies that the *junta* had been forced to seek refuge in Cádiz and that the future seemed bleak, American leaders in several of the provinces felt that the time had come to break definitively with the mother country presumed to be in the power of the French. This was the situation which the independence-minded among them had hoped for.

● **The Revolutions: A General Observation**

The drive for independence had much the same motivation and inspiration everywhere in Latin America. The implementation of that drive varied from area to area. The colonials universally had grievances stemming out of overregulation, oppressive taxation, social discrimination, and general refusal of mother countries to accept the ideas of the new age.

Although there was an early push for social change in New Spain, in most of the areas, and ultimately also in Mexico, the prime goal of the leaders was political change. These leaders, regularly *criollos,* seemed satisfied to force out the *peninsulares* and to take over their positions. They talked loudly and persuasively of democracy, liberty, and equality, and wrote constitutions incorporating these ideals. However, once on top it became evident that they wanted little more in the way of change than simple political turnover. Secure in their new position of leadership, they very quickly forgot their inflammatory rhetoric and also their mestizo, mulatto, and Indian allies of the fighting days. In time they would see that these benefits were shared by all, but they would be the judges of the proper time and the extent of the sharing. The *criollos* became the new aristocracy.

● **The Wars in Northern South America**

Venezuela and Nueva Granada. Caracas, birthplace of Francisco de Miranda, the "Precursor," and of Simón Bolívar, the "Liberator," was an important focal point of agitation shortly after word of the 1810 events in Spain reached the Americas. A *cabildo abierto* (town meeting), called in April, voted to break with the Junta Central in Spain, which it was feared might already be defunct, and to form a local governing *junta* to rule in the name of Ferdinand VII. The next year the Sociedad Patriótica summoned a convention to draft a constitution. In July 1811, under the leadership of Miranda, this body declared independence and established the First Venezuelan Republic.

That government lasted not quite a year. In March of 1812 the country was shaken by a severe earthquake, which, curiously and somewhat ominously, did heaviest damage in the rebel eastern provinces and almost none in the loyal west. This was taken as a sign of divine punishment of disloyalty and the so-called earthquake republic collapsed. Bolívar and other younger leaders, disenchanted with Miranda, bought safe conduct out of the country by betraying the "Precursor" into the hands of the royalist commander at La Guaira, General Juan Domingo Monteverde. Miranda had previously angered Spain by his abortive attempt to rouse the country in 1806. Happy to have him in their custody, the Spanish authorities sent him off to Spain, where he was imprisoned and died in a Spanish dungeon, a broken and disillusioned man.

Meanwhile, patriots in Nueva Granada (Colombia) had reacted in similar fashion to the news of 1810 from Spain. There was a *cabildo abierto* in Bogotá and a declaration of independence, but strong disagreement over the kind of constitution to be drafted split the participants. Those from Bogotá, the Bogotanos, wanted a strong centralist government, with their city as capital. The federalists thereupon withdrew to Tunja and took over the revolutionary movement. When Bolívar, a refugee from Venezuela, came to Nueva Granada with the aim of continuing the war against Spain, he accepted a commission from the Tunja regime, campaigned successfully in the Magdalena valley, and then with Granadine assistance turned eastward to liberate once again his native Venezuela. In 1814 a Second Venezuelan Republic was proclaimed, but like its precedessor did not last long. By mid-1814 Caracas and all Venezuela were again firmly under royalist control.

The tide began to turn in 1817. The irrepressible Bolívar was back still another time, on this occasion with his famous "British Legion," English veterans of the Napoleonic wars whom he had recruited. On this occasion the "Liberator" landed far to the east, made contact with Páez, swept through the Orinoco Valley and across the Andes into Nueva Granada, which Francisco Paula de Santander was winning back from the royalists. Together, they administered a crushing defeat to the royalists, in August 1819, at Boyacá, high in the northern Andes. Later in that year Nueva Granada and the liberated Venezuelan provinces joined in the new state of Gran Colombia, at Angostura. In June 1821 Bolívar bested General Miguel de la Torre at Carabobo. This marked the end of royalist power in the north.

Ecuador. Meanwhile, Bolívar's crack lieutenant, Antonio José de Sucre, reputedly the best general of the period, had fought his way south from Nueva Granada into Ecuador. On the slopes of the great volcano which towers over Quito, in May 1822, Sucre, with help from José de San Martín, already in Peru, won the decisive Battle of Pichincha and clinched independence for the entire north. Ecuador then joined the Confederation of Gran Colombia.

● The Wars in Southern South America

Argentina. In the south, too, word of the events of 1810 in Spain touched off the revolutionary movement. In Buenos Aires a *cabildo abierto,* reluctantly summoned by the viceroy, voted on May 22 to depose that officer and to vest control in the hands of a governing *junta.* In 1811 the *junta* was disbanded in favor of a triumvirate, which was soon replaced by another three-man team. This latter included two strong leaders recently returned to their homeland, José de San Martín and Carlos de Alvear.

In 1813 a constituent assembly gathered and drafted a first constitution for the United Provinces of La Plata. It put the executive power in the hands of a supreme director, and Gervasio Posadas was first to hold that office. Troubles with Uruguay and José Gervasio Artigas led to the resignation of Posadas. His nephew, Carlos Alvear, was his successor, but, again, not for long. Next, in the scramble for power Alvear was overturned and the *cabildo* of Buenos Aires took charge. This body called for a general congress of all the provinces. It met in 1817 at Tucumán, made the first formal declaration of independence, named Juan de Pueyrredón supreme director, and proceeded to draft a constitution. When this document was finished in 1818 and presented to the nation, the provinces found it too centralist in character and much too pro-Buenos Aires. As a result they refused to accept it. This sort of scrambling for power and internal dissension continued for a dozen more years, until a strong man, Juan Manuel de Rosas, arose to impose his brand of unity on the nation.

Paraguay. Despite its landlocked location and consequent geographic dependence on Argentina for access to the outside world, Paraguayan leaders received the Argentina invitation to join with the larger province in the break from Spain very coolly. When there seemed some likelihood that Buenos Aires might force the issue, Paraguay declared her own independence, and under the domineering leadership of José Gaspar Francia became a nation.

Uruguay. This other small nation of the southern group ran a much less smooth course to national independence. Her champion José Gervasio Artigas first opposed the incorporation designs of the Argentines. Next he brought down on himself and his little country the wrath of the Portuguese who, in 1818, invaded this so-called Banda Oriental, took Montevideo, drove out Artigas in 1820, and annexed the area to Brazil as the Cisplatine Province. When Argentina challenged, war broke out between Argentina and Brazil. Not until 1828, and then largely through the interposition of Great Britain, did Uruguay win independence as a separate nation rather than as part of its larger neighbors.

● **Beyond the Andes**

Chile. Chile had a long and often bloody fight for independence. In 1810 news out of Spain precipitated patriot action in Santiago, the capital. By September the royal officials had been deposed in favor of a local *junta*. The next year a national congress took charge, dominated by the Carrera brothers, especially José Miguel who quickly tried to rule as a dictator. Word of the ensuing internal strife within patriot ranks prompted the viceroy of Peru, José Fernando Abascal, to act. General Antonio Pareja, dispatched southward with a sizable force, easily took possession of the Isle of Chiloé and thence moved north to Concepción. This royalist invasion for the moment united the patriots.

The ultimate hope for Chile, however, was even then shaping up on the farther side of the Andes. The Argentine José de San

Martín had returned to his native land in 1811, after years abroad during which he developed dreams of independence for Latin America. He had been temporarily involved in the political struggles in Buenos Aires but was soon sent north as military commander, to put to work the expertise acquired during his European years. He quickly recognized the futility of trying to take Peru overland. He asked to be relieved of his military command and to be allowed to serve his country, instead, as governor of Cuyo, the Argentine province on the eastern slope of the cordillera. His hope was, operating from that base, first to drive the Spaniards out of Chile and then from this new base to move against Peru by sea. As governor of Cuyo, he quietly convinced his friend Supreme Director Juan Pueyrredón of the soundness of his strategy and won valuable aid, while far out beyond the *pampa* he went about assembling, training, and equipping an army at Mendoza, the capital of Cuyo. Some of the Chilean leaders-in-exile, notably Bernardo O'Higgins, joined him at Mendoza.

By January 1817, San Martín was ready to move his little army across the towering Andes. His misinformers, sent ahead, succeeded in confusing the Spaniards as to his intentions, with the result that the three divisions of the patriot force were able to rendezvous at San Felipe, without royal challenge. This new Army of Chile won a smashing victory at Chacabuco on February 12. Two days later San Martín and Bernardo O'Higgins entered Santiago in triumph. Although pressed by the jubilant populace to take the post, San Martín deferred to O'Higgins, who became the first Supreme Director of independent Chile. The new government suffered a temporary setback at Cancha Rayada in 1818 but quickly bounced back to crush the Spaniards at Maipú. As of April 1818, Chile was independent.

The Two Perus. The heart of the old viceroyalty of Peru was the next patriot objective. All realized that until Spain was definitely pushed out of Lima, the highland, and off the *altiplano* of Upper Peru, the independence of all of Latin America could never be a sure thing.

Preparations for the attack on Peru by sea got under way immediately. San Martín crossed back to Argentina for funds and assistance but was rebuffed by the new government there and was actually ordered home with his force. He refused and went back to Chile. As the time for the departure of the developing fleet neared, the patriots had the singular good fortune to enlist the services of Thomas Cochrane as their admiral. Cochrane, an extraordinarily able seaman but an explosive personality, had quarreled with his former British superiors and been dismissed from His Majesty's Navy. Interested in the cause of Latin American independence since the days in 1806 when he had unofficially helped Miranda during the premature landing on the Venezuelan shore, he was now happy to devote time to the new adventure.

The little Chilean armada sailed out of Valparaiso in August 1820. San Martín landed a detachment of his force at Pisco, then himself disembarked with the rest of the army farther north, and left Cochrane at sea to worry the Spaniards off Callao. At this point the royalist forces, under their generals José de La Serna and José Canterac, withdrew into the high country. San Martín, who had no desire to come as a conqueror waited near Lima until the Limeños invited his assistance. In July 1821 he entered the "Ciudad de los Reyes" by invitation and the *cabildo* named him "Protector." For almost a year little happened. The patriots held Lima, Callao, and several coastal cities, but the royalists were in secure possession of the high interior. A stalemate was developing.

Then, in July 1822, came the famous conference at Guayaquil between the two giants of the liberation movement, San Martín and Bolívar. When marked disagreements showed between the two leaders, San Martín, now a very sick and discouraged man, decided to withdraw and leave the final mop-up to the younger and more aggressive Bolívar, making sure that personal rivalries did not harm the great cause.

Bolívar had to return north to face growing problems in his Gran Colombia. Taking advantage of this leaderless interlude in Peru, La Serna and Canterac came down from the high country and soon had Lima and all Peru, Callao excepted, again under royal control. Desperate, the patriots brought Bolívar south and named him dictator and commander-in-chief. In August 1824, he routed Canterac at Junín and in December his capable lieutenant Sucre crushed the Spaniards at Ayacucho.

Upper Peru was Spain's last province, but now only weakly held. Sucre went up to the *altiplano* and by August 1825 had complete control of the country. The next year Bolívar gave the new nation a constitution, and in gratitude that nation took his name and became Bolivia. Thus as of 1826 the Spanish Empire in South America was no more, an era had come to an end.

● **New Spain Becomes Mexico**

The Hidalgo Movement. A group of conspirators in Querétaro, with Padre Miguel Hidalgo, parish priest of nearby Dolores, as a leading force, planned revolutionary action for December 1810. In September there was a leak and the royal authorities learned something of what was going on and prepared to take action. A revolutionary plot at Valladolid, uncovered the year before, had put the viceregal government on the alert. The night of September 15 the warning came to Hidalgo, at the moment in Dolores with one of his coconspirators, Ignacio Allende. Before midnight the decision to act immediately was made, in order to anticipate government action and arrest. The next day was Sunday. Hidalgo turned his sermon of the day into the "Grito de Dolores," a rousing call to his parishioners to strike for freedom and to drive out the Spaniards, the *gachupines* (those with spurs or the upper class of *peninsulares*). This day is still celebrated as Mexico's official independence day. A motley army of poorly armed Indians, mestizos, and a few *criollos* later that morning headed for nearby San Miguel, where the royal garrison joined the force. Next was Celaya, where more joined. Then the "army" moved to Guanajuato, capital of the *intendencia*. Here the movement showed a definite racial character, when the whites were butchered and the town sacked.

Drunk with blood and success the revolutionaries headed toward Mexico City picking up more adherents as they slowly proceeded. En route they defeated a small royal force sent by the viceroy to stop them. Within striking distance of the viceregal capital, Hidalgo had second thoughts and became seriously afraid that he would be unable to control the force which he had unleashed, that he might have a second and more terrible Guanajuato on his conscience. Therefore, he ordered a withdrawal to friendly Guadalajara in order to regroup and organize. En route General Félix Calleja caught up with the retreating horde and administered a telling blow. Even so, Hidalgo and his dwindling "army" made Guadalajara, where he was hailed as liberator and attempted to form a government. Calleja came on with a force of seven thousand disciplined troops. Allende counseled a further withdrawal to the definitely prorebel north, which a campaigning Mariano Jiménez had largely won to the cause. Hidalgo, trusting in his many thousands, welcomed the confrontation. That decision

was a sorry mistake. His "army" was completely routed. The leaders scattered, heading for refuge in the province of Texas, which also was reported as sympathetic. They were intercepted, taken, and executed. The heads of the four ringleaders, Hidalgo, Allende, Jiménez, and Juan Aldama, fixed on pikes, were put on the four corners of the granary of Guanajuato, the scene of the worst butchery of a few months before.

The Morelos Action. Another priest, José María Morelos, former pupil during Hidalgo's term as a seminary professor, heard the "Grito de Dolores," and set out to rouse the country to the west and south of the capital. A more competent leader than Hidalgo, he kept the movement alive until 1815, with the aid of such *insurgente* chieftains as Vicente Guerrero. At Chilpancingo, in 1813, Morelos and his associates issued the first Mexican declaration of independence. But in the end Morelos, like his former mentor, was captured, defrocked, and executed. As of 1815 the revolt in New Spain seemed to be dead. However, the seed sown would soon sprout, but in a somewhat different fashion.

Independence with Iturbide. The first Mexican movements had too many racial and lower-class aspects to win the sympathetic support of the *criollos*. No matter how earnestly they might desire independence, they wanted it their own way, with themselves, not the masses, calling the tune. Consequently during the recent disturbances they had, as a group, supported the viceregal and royal party of law and order. They seemed willing to bide their time.

Then events in Spain awakened new worries in *criollos* in Mexico and turned them into potential revolutionaries. Ferdinand VII back on the Spanish throne was comporting himself more and more as an absolutist of the old stamp. In 1820 the Spanish liberals took a stand in what was known as the Riego Revolt. They demanded that Ferdinand return in practice to the Constitution of 1812, which he had promised to uphold. This constitution, put together in the days of the threatened takeover by the French invaders of the peninsula, was patterned after the French Revolutionary Constitution of 1791. It set up a limited monarch who very definitely was to share power with a representative body of the citizenry; the Spanish Cortes of 1820 felt that Ferdinand was not doing this, and the numerous liberals in the Cortes wanted the situation righted. One of their first acts after achieving this goal was to declare that the Constitution of 1812 was the organic law not only for the mother country but for the remaining overseas provinces as well.

When apprized of this decision, leadership elements in Mexican society became much concerned. The great majority of *criollos*, inclined to be political conservatives, were profoundly worried over the prospect of having their lives dominated by homeland liberals. Leading Mexican churchmen, aware of the anticlerical overtones of the Constitution, feared that these might be activated by a liberal Cortes. Maybe independence offered the best protection.

In this atmosphere of apprehension Agustín Iturbide emerged as a leader. A native of Valladolid (Mexico), he was a *criollo* and, further, he had a military record, having fought against Hidalgo, Morelos, and the guerrilla *insurgentes*; he also was ambitious. With his *Plan de Iguala* he managed to rally all factions in support of its "three guarantees"—Mexico, having broken with the mother country, would be a constitutional monarchy, with Ferdinand VII or at least a Bourbon as the prince; all Mexicans, *criollos*, mestizos, Indians, *castas* of every blood strain, would have equal rights; and, finally, the Roman Catholic religion, to the exclusion of all others, would be the state creed. The *Plan*, as is evident, had something for everyone. The country rallied behind Iturbide, defied the Cortes, and proclaimed independence.

When Spain sent a new viceroy to carry out the orders of the Cortes, Iturbide met this Don Juan O'Donojú at Vera Cruz. The pair withdrew to the more salubrious site of Córdoba, in the hills away from the steaming port. O'Donojú quickly recognized the state of the situation and the temper of the Mexicans. Realistically, he agreed to the so-called Treaty of Córdoba which called for a recognition of Mexican independence. The Cortes disavowed the action of its agent, but it was too late. Mexico had already begun to act as a sovereign nation. The date was 1821.

● **Central America**

The five provinces (Guatemala, El Salvador, Honduras, Nicaragua, Costa Rica) which in colonial times had made up the old captaincy-general of Guatemala, adopted a similar stance. They ousted the royal officials and rallied behind local leaders. For a short time Mexico sought to annex these provinces, but Central

Americans soon determined among themselves to go their own way, as a confederation.

● The Caribbean

The independence movement did not spread to the Spanish Caribbean Islands, such as Puerto Rico and Cuba, which remained loyal and experienced no revolts. They continued as colonies of Spain into the next century.

● Independence for Brazil

The road to nationhood for Brazil, Portugal's single American colony, was different. Brazil did have rumblings of discontent in the later eighteenth century, for example the Tiradentes uprising in the backcountry, led by young Joaquim José da Silva Xavier. There was an awareness of the tempting new ideas of the Age of the Enlightenment, but dissatisfaction was not as acute as in the Spanish colonies. A peculiar set of circumstances would heighten that discontent and turn it into a drive for independence.

The Arrival of the Royal Family. When early in 1808 the refugee royal party, with some thousands of nobles accompanying the queen and Regent João, spirited out of Portugal by the British, arrived in Bahía, a new era opened for Brazil. Dom João, who in time succeeded his ailing mother as sovereign, immediately liked Brazil and Brazilians. Shocked by the appalling lack of interest toward the colony by his predecessors, Dom João instituted many reforms, some of these even before the royal party moved from Bahía to Rio de Janeiro, much to the delight of the colonials of the capital. In 1815 King João VI took the unprecedented step of raising Brazil to the rank of a kingdom, equal in status to Portugal itself. Such recognition made it a bit easier for the Brazilians to put up with the increasing insolence of their less-than-appreciative guests, the nobles in exile.

Toward Independence. With the winds of revolt blowing through the Spanish provinces all around, it was inevitable that the Brazilians should be affected. When João, under pressure from the Portuguese Cortes, went back to rule from the mother country in 1821, he left his son Dom Pedro as regent in Brazil.

Departing, João sagely advised his son that, if a drive for independence developed, he, Dom Pedro, should head rather than attempt to thwart the movement. Wily João thought thus to retain the American province as part of the patrimony of the House of Braganza.

Having gotten the king back, the next move of the Portuguese Cortes was to bring Dom Pedro back as well and to reduce Brazil once again to its "proper" status as a colony. Dom Pedro answered the first summons with his statement that he would remain in Brazil, "if it be for the good of all and for the general felicity of the nation."

The next summons from the Cortes was even more peremptory. Dom Pedro's so-called "Grito de Ypiranga" (Independence or death!) was his unequivocal answer. Brazil dates her independence from that day, September 7, 1822.

Separation from the mother country was in the main bloodless. There was no serious attempt on the part of Portugal to change the determination of the Brazilians by force of arms. Some royal garrisons made a show of resistance, but this was met by Dom Pedro with some slight armed action and much personal persuasion. He soon issued the call for a convention to furnish a constitution for the new nation. All agreed that the government should be a constitutional monarchy, even though they favored "The Empire of Brazil" as the official name of the country.

Within a few years Portugal herself formally recognized the situation and accepted Brazil as a fellow nation in the world family. This sort of understanding preserved a warmth between the former colony and the former mother country. Spain would have been well advised to have been as tolerant and forgiving toward her departing American children—hard feelings on both sides endured a long time.

Conclusion

As of 1826 eighteen new nations, the Latin Americas, had recently joined the world family—two more, Cuba and Panama, would join later. They were independent, on their own. Whether ready for the challenge or not, their destinies would be of their own making. The days of colonial dependence were no more. But these colonial centuries, the growing-up years, had great importance and were largely responsible in preparing them for their future. Events and experiences, attitudes and outlooks acquired, strengths and weaknesses developed, all those colonial things, had become a part of each.

Suggestions for Further Reading

Bannon, John Francis, *The Spanish Borderlands Frontier, 1513-1821*. New York: Holt, Rinehart and Winston, 1970. [North America]

Caruso, John A., *The Liberators of Mexico*. Gloucester, Mass.: P. Smith, 1954.

Crow, John A., *The Epic of Latin America*, revised. New York: Doubleday, 1971.

Descola, Jean, *The Conquistadors*, tr. by Malcolm Barnes. New York: Viking, 1957.

Freyre, Gilberto, *The Masters and the Slaves*, tr. by Samuel Putname. New York: Knopf, 1956. [Brazil]

Gibson, Charles, *Spain in America*. New York: Harper & Row, 1966.

Goodman, Edward J., *The Explorers of South America*. New York: Macmillan, 1972.

Haring, Clarence H., *The Spanish Empire in America*, revised. New York: Harcourt, Brace, Jovanovich, 1952.

Kinsbruner, Jay, *The Spanish-American Independence Movement*. Hillsdale, Ill.: Dryden, 1973.

Leonard, Irving A., *Baroque Times in Old Mexico*. Ann Arbor: University of Michigan Press, 1959.

Means, Philip A., *The Fall of the Inca Empire and Spanish Rule in Peru, 1530-1780*. New York: Scribners, 1932.

———*The Spanish Main: Focus of Envy, 1492-1700*. New York: Scribners, 1935.

Parry, John H., *The Age of Reconnaissance*. Cleveland: World, 1955.

Prado, Caio, Jr., *The Colonial Background of Modern Brazil*, tr. by Suzette Macedo. Berkeley: University of California Press, 1967.

Schurz, William L., *This New World*. New York: Dutton, 1954.

Shiels, W. Eugene, *King and Church: The Rise and Fall of the Patronato Real*. Chicago: Loyola University Press, 1961.

Stein, Stanley J. and Barbara H., *The Colonial Heritage of Latin America*. New York: Oxford University Press, 1970.

Wauchope, Robert, *The Indian Background of Latin American History: The Maya, Aztec, Inca, and Their Predecessors*. New York, Knopf, 1970.

Zavala, Silvio, *New Viewpoints on the Spanish Colonization of America*. Philadelphia: University of Pennsylvania Press, 1943.

Glossary

adelantado—title given to an individual in the early period of the Indies named to conquer and rule an area

alcabala—crown's sales tax

alcalde mayor—ranking officer in a Spanish town, "mayor"

alcalde ordinario—town judge, justice of the peace

alférez—standard-bearer in town pageantry, some towns proudly had royal coats of arms

alguacil—equivalently the town chief of police

armada de barlovento—coast guard in the Caribbean

asiento—a royal contract

ayuntamiento—a variant name for the town *cabildo*

bandeirantes—Portuguese of the south ranging into the interior in search of slaves and riches

barrio—the proper district of a town

cabildo—town council

cabildo abierto—open town meeting

cacique—Indian chieftain or ruler

capitulación—contract

castas—the colored groups in colonial society

caudillo—a dictator, generally a military man, more common in the national period

colegio—intermediate institution in educational system, equivalent to high school plus junior college

conquistador—Spanish conqueror in the Americas

cordillera—a geographic term meaning mountain range, specifically used to designate the Andean ranges of South America

corregidor—the ranking official, generally in an Indian town

criollo—Spaniard-born in the Indies, a creole in the historical sense

donatario—a Portuguese to whom the crown made a captaincy grant

encomienda—an assignment of Indians to a meriting conquistador who became their protector and the beneficiary of the tribute they otherwise owed to the crown

fazenda—a Portuguese/Brazilian sugar plantation

flota—Spanish merchant fleet operating to and from the Indies in armed convoy *gachupines*—"men with spurs," uncomplimentary term applied to Spaniards in the day of the war for independence (Mexico)

gaucho—cowboy of the Argentine-Uruguayan pampa

gente de razón—"folk of reason," name given to whites and near-whites in colonial society

hacienda—a landed estate

hidalgo—gentleman, lower level of the nobility

insurgentes—guerrilla chieftains in early drive for Mexican independence

intendencia—new administrative unit introduced into Indies in the late eighteenth century

llanero—cowboy of the Venezuelan backcountry

llanos—the lush plains of the Venezuelan backcountry in the Orinoco valley

mestizo—offspring of union of European and Indian

mita—the *repartimiento* known by this name in areas of South America

montaña—eastern slope of the Andes

mulatto—offspring of European and African

navío de permiso—the cargo ship permitted to call at designated ports in the Indies following the Treaty of Utrecht (1713)

obrage—workshop (textile) to which Indians were assigned for work by the *repartimiento* detail

oriente—eastern slope of the Andes

paisanos—the nonmissionary, nonmilitary Spanish settlers on the frontier

pampa—lush grassy plains of Argentina and Uruguay

Patronato Real—the right of royal patronage over the church

peninsular—a Spaniard born in the mother country (the Iberian peninsula)

presidio—a frontier fort with small garrison

quinto—crown tax on treasure collected and mined, one fifth or 20 percent

Real Hacienda—the royal treasury of a viceroyalty or province

reductions—Indian missions by the Jesuits in Paraguay

regidor—member of the *cabildo* or town council, initially popularly elected

repartimiento—apportionment of Indians in work detail, assigned by a royal officer

residencia—official review of the service of an outgoing official in the Indies, conducted by a royally appointed *juez* (judge)

tithe—the ecclesiastical tax (one tenth) of the income/wealth of Spanish subject

vaquero—cowboy of New Spain

viceroy—the ranking royal official in the Indies

visitador—a royally appointed agent sent to the Indies on a specific mission whose authority generally superseded that of the viceroy during his presence in the Indies

zambo—offspring of the union of Indian and African, regularly carried the social taint of the slave parent

Index